COMPILED AND EDITED BY

JEFF MENZISE, PH.D.

FOREWORD BY

MOLEFI K. ASANTE, PH.D.

For information address Mind on the Matter Publishing, Post Office Box 755, College Park, Maryland 20741.

10 9 8 7 6 5 4 3

Cover Design by Jeffery Menzise, Ph.D.

Library of Congress Cataloging-in-Publication Data
Menzise, Jeffery,
Rambling Ruminations: Rare Writings from the Collection of J. A. Rogers/ Edited by Jeffery Menzise, Ph.D. Includes Cover Artwork & Design, and Foreword by Molefi K. Asante, Ph.D.

ISBN 978-0-9856657-1-5

Published in 2013 by
Mind on the Matter Publishing,
P.O. Box 755, College Park, MD 20741
Website: www.mindonthematter.com
Email: drjeff@mindonthematter.com
240-988-9639 office

Acknowledgements

I would like to thank my Ancestors for their continued support and guidance as I strive to live on purpose. I also want to thank Morgan State University and the Institute for Urban Research for their support while completing this project. Additionally, special thanks goes to Fisk University's Special Collections where the late Mrs. Helga Rogers has trusted the personal collection of her husband Joel Augustus Rogers. Finally I would like to thank my family for their patience and support while I worked diligently to resurrect the voice of the great J. A. Rogers.

Dedication

This book is dedicated to the wonderful memory of Ms. Beth Madison Howse, the angel who, for so many years as a true daughter of Fisk University, remained "e'er on the alter." She, like Mr. J. A. Rogers, served as the protector and preserver of our ancestral legacy by standing guard over the Special Collections at Fisk University. True to her love for history and tradition, Ms. Howse lovingly assisted thousands of scholars seeking to navigate the priceless collection left to her care. With her warm heart and gentle smile, she would greet me daily as I worked on this project. Thank you Ms. Howse, I could not have completed this task without you.

"As was generally the case, J. A. Rogers came across information, publicized it, was considered controversial and way off base in his statements and conclusions. Then subsequent research found him to be correct and could go beyond it, thereby validating it...In his research all over the world, by looking at the artifacts first-hand, he compiled a body of history as a pioneer, with all the glories and drawbacks of a pioneer, decades ahead of his time, a work that will stand as his monument and will have to be referred to in any U.S. teaching of "integrated" history, integrated in the proper meaning of the word, history taught in its proper perspective, without trying to gloss over historical facts for one reason or another..."

"He did more than anyone else in the field, and had his writings been heeded, maybe we would not have the awful mess with our schools, with the inner cities."

Mrs. Helga M. Rogers, 1995
Biographical Sketch
100 Amazing Facts About
the Negro with Complete Proof

Table of Contents

FOREWORD

As a child growing up in Valdosta, Georgia I remember my father reaching under his bed and pulling out a thin paperback book. It was J. A. Rogers' Five Black Presidents. My father would tell us stories of great black queens and kings who created civilizations long before there was a United States of America. He would regale us with lofty ideas of music invented by the swarthy Beethoven or elevate us with pride by speaking of Alexander Dumas and the Three Musketeers. Like many African Americans of the 1940s and 1950s my early consciousness was raised by attaching myself to the narratives of power and victory in J. A. Rogers' books.

Rogers was like an itinerant preacher traveling from city to city with his special words of power based on his study of the African past. He knew that the people needed what he was writing and he was among the most motivated to discover the insatiable desire that blacks had for information about history. Joel Augustus Rogers was born in Negril, Jamaica on September 6, 1883 and lived until 1966. When he came to the United States in 1906, Jamaica was still a British colony and Marcus Garvey had not yet made it to Harlem. It would be ten years later that the most famous Jamaican would enter the United States. Nevertheless, Rogers understood as much as any other black person during his lifetime that it was necessary to fight the perception that Africans had no history. He did not allow his mixed racial origin to quench his thirst for knowledge. He abhorred the idea that whites were superior to other races and set out to prove that they had falsified African history. He once said that when he was in school he observed that some of his classmates who were purely Africans were more brilliant than those who were whites. During the year that he became a naturalized American citizen, 1917, he published his first book, From Superman to Man, and it immediately made a mark in the discussions about race.

Others had preceded him in the work of uncovering the mythic nature of African achievement but few had understood as clearly as Rogers the true nature of the propaganda. As the Germans were expounding their ideology of National Socialism through their Propagandaministerium J. A. Rogers was making his books the black thrust into the world of knowledge, history, science, and belief. If he had not appeared when he did there would have had to be someone else like him because the African populations needed his lay interpretations and presentations of the truth of our history.

While the Trinidadian Henry Sylvester Williams and the African American W. E. B. Du Bois advanced the concept of Pan Africanism and the Jamaican Marcus Garvey preached Africa for Africans at home and abroad, it would be J. A. Rogers who through his deliberate, rational, and relentless work who demonstrated the interconnectedness of all people of African descent. Williams held the first Pan African Conference in London in 1911 and Du Bois would feature in five Pan African Congresses and Garvey would articulate a fierce nationalism when he arrived in New York in 1916, but Rogers would listen to their voices and others and take up his intellectual sword, using his skill as a researcher and avid bibliophile, to hack his way through the confusion about our history and culture in order to establish the truth of this or that fact.

Consequently, J. A. Rogers popularized information about Alexander Pushkin, Alexander Dumas, and the five black presidents. The aha moment of realization struck us every time we would read a new fact about some black composer in England or some relatively unknown African person in Asia who achieved something remarkable. With Rogers' books and pamphlets it was almost always a feeling the he would uncover something that would make you stand taller and sit more erect because you knew almost intuitively that what he was saying was true. It was in opposition to the propaganda about African inferiority and lack of achievement that Rogers used his sword. Whether the author was commenting on black Catholic Popes or Caesars or inventors he remained committed to teaching us that our history had been stolen and locked into books scattered over the world in many languages. It was J. A. Rogers' ambition to reveal what had been concealed.

Of course, Rogers soon began to examine in detail the European bloodlines and discovered to the amazement of many people that many of the most famous "white" people had African ancestry! Thus, the Pullman Car porter who had studied art for a while in Chicago made his mark on the society with books that were thoroughly illustrated to make his points. The book, Nature Knows No Color-Line and the three volume collection, Sex and Race, contested every argument of Aryan race superiority. Once he had completed his denouncing and debunking white racial arrogance he set about to write a compendium of The World's Greatest Men of African Descent in 1931. In 1947 the book, The World's Great Men of Color from 3000 BC to 1946 AD, brought him additional fame and respect throughout the African world.

Rogers found every excuse to use his travels on the train to investigate the libraries, private book collections, and bookstores featuring people of African origin. I have known many people like Rogers in my time. They do not just love the collection of materials about African people, they are passionate, driven in their desire to uncover information about the grand journey of the African people. These lay guerilla fighters for information have been praised heroes in our communities, though not necessarily have they been people who are known by the educated elite of African Americans. However, John Henrik Clarke, Arturo Schomburg, Ed Robinson, Yosef Ben-Jochannon, Hubert Harrison, Chancellor Williams, William Leo Hansberry, Ivan Van Sertima, and others stood beside, and often on the shoulders of, J. A. Rogers and together made a phalanx of race men who could not allow black people's history to be forgotten. He died on March 26, 1966 having left an indelible imprint on the discourse on identity in the world.

Molefi Kete Asante is Professor and Chair, Department of African American Studies, at Temple University. Asante is the author of 76 books, Including The African American People: A Global History.

Image 1. J. A. Rogers as an elder in his NYC bookstore.

PREFACE

The year was 1999 and I was visiting Africa for the first time. My first step on the continent was in Dakar, Senegal. I was with a group of students representing various universities on a study abroad trip to The Gambia in West Africa. This trip was the highlight of my four years at Fisk University and seemed to be the perfect and logical next step in my newly found journey towards reclaiming my African-Self Identity. I had just graduated with my Bachelor's degree in psychology and was returning to Fisk in the Fall to begin a Master of Arts degree in clinical psychology, a decision that prompted me to work with the Ministry of Education and the West African Examination Council in Gambia's capital city, Banjul.

It was during one of my long hot walks after exiting the bus from Bakau to Banjul that I stumbled upon a street vendor, literally sitting on the dusty curb with several books scattered across a blanket. Far be it from me to walk past someone selling books without at least taking a look. Of the at least twenty books to choose from, three stood out the most: Volumes 1 and III of J. A. Rogers' Sex and Race, and a copy of the Tibetan Book of the Dead. At the time, the Tibetan Book of the Dead seemed to carry the most relevance because I had recently began to explore the spiritual legacy of my Ancestors and was deep into what I then called "The Egyptian Book of the Dead" and various other ancient texts dealing with spiritual growth and development. The two J. A. Rogers volumes stood out because I had seen them many times at our local African Bookstore in

Nashville (Alkebu-lan Images and Books), and knew that he was a man that was to be respected in regards to his writings on Africa and her children.

For some strange reason I was more surprised to see his books in Gambia than I was to find the Tibetan Book of the Dead; needless to say, I now better understand how in-place his books are on the continent of Africa. I purchased the three books and kept them close the entire trip. I began reading the Tibetan Book of the Dead, and simply packed Mr. Rogers' books among the other books I brought along with me to Africa (including Some's Of Water and the Spirit, Amen's Metu Neter vols. 1 and 2, and a few of Muata Ashby's Egyptian Yoga books).

On our way back to Dakar, one of my fellow travelers asked if she could read the Tibetan Book of the Dead and return it to me on the flight. I have yet to see that book again; as for the two volumes of Sex and Race, I have kept them and have only lent them out once to an older cousin. Oddly, I have never purchased volume two, feeling that even if I purchased the second volume, my set would not be complete...I'd need to buy all three together for that.

I now find myself 13 years later embarking on this journey to uncover and share with the world some of J. A. Rogers writings from the 1920s and 1930s, communications that few of us still living have ever read. I am sure of this because they were published in various newspapers and publications in those decades and have since vanished into obscurity. The way that our ancestor's work has always amazed me. In this case, I was led back to Mr. Rogers' works right there on the campus of Fisk University, in a library that I have spent many nights studying and days socializing with my friends, and listening to the stories of Dr. Leslie (L. M.) Collins. One of my colleagues Mr. Uzoma Miller was working on staff in Special Collections and was in the process of doing inventory on "The Garvey Papers," which itself was/is amazing to me. I then inquired further into the breadth and depth of our collection at Fisk, that is when I learned that J. A. Rogers' personal papers, travel journals, correspondences, etc. had been donated to Fisk by his wife, the late Mrs. Helga M. Rogers for safe keeping.

I declared in that moment that I would begin this quest to compile the writings of J. A. Rogers and share them with the world. I didn't realize how much this journey would change my life. Literally reading from his travel journals, browsing his private photos (some of which are actually used in the collage on the cover of the Sex and Race volumes), and reading his letters from historical giants like George A. Padmore, Amy Jacques Garvey, and his wife Helga, I got a rare and life changing jolt; feeling for the first time such a powerful and real connection with a legacy that spans decades, centuries, millenia and generations.

My prayer is that you, the reader, will get at least a portion of the excitement that I received as I transcribed these articles for the compilation of Rambling Ruminations.

Jeffery Menzise, Ph.D.
30,000 feet above Earth
En Route to Baltimore

PART 1: RAMBLING RUMINATIONS

The various articles found in this collection come from a variety of sources, all of which were mined over a three year period by the editor, Dr. Jeff Menzise. In the first section, our readers will find as an introduction to J. A. Rogers' perspective, an excerpt from an undated article from A. Phillip Randolph's "The Messenger" which was found as a clipping in the personal archives of Mr. Rogers held at Fisk University. The remainder of the first section of ***Rambling Ruminations*** are articles that Mr. Rogers published for the Pittsburgh Courier between February of 1926 and September of 1927. These articles cover a variety of topics from the African presence in various European nations to his visit with Mr. Marcus Mosiah Garvey while incarcerated in an Atlanta prison. Many current day followers of J. A. Rogers have never read these articles due to the fact that they were published in newspapers in the mid-1920s; it is my hopes that by offering these articles in one volume, the reader will find a treasure trove of information and research perspective to help their understanding of Mr. Rogers and the times of which he writes.

In the second section of ***Rambling Ruminations***, the reader is treated to the running column from which this book derives its name. In addition to writing for the Pittsburgh Courier, Mr. Rogers also wrote articles for the New York Amsterdam News called "Rambling Ruminations" (sometimes abbreviated as "Ruminations"). The articles presented in this collection are transcribed from newspaper clippings found in the personal collection of J. A. Rogers found in the Special Collections of Fisk University. When filing these clippings of his articles, Mr. Rogers did not include the actual dates of publication, and thus, they are not included here. This fact helps to illustrate the timeless nature of J. A. Rogers' perspective and writings; as you read on, you will see that, aside from certain references made to the then current events and persons living during those times, many of his articles are as relevant and applicable here in the 21st century as they were when initially written.

As you read, imagine that you are in Harlem, USA in the 1920s and 30s, in the throws of the Harlem Renaissance. Imagine that you are awakening to your racial identity as an African descendant here in the United States of America and that Joel Augustus Rogers is the courier, the messenger, the one responsible for delivering to you, the facts of race and race relations around the world. Imagine the eagerness with which many must have awaited the next article to be featured in the Pittsburgh Courier or the New York Amsterdam News proclaiming that Africans are seen as more than former slaves by the majority of peoples around the planet. Imagine as you read his descriptions of the Rock of Gibraltar, Mount Vesuvius and Morocco how exciting it must have been to hear of such wonders of the world.

Allow yourself to ruminate with J. A. Rogers, as he shares his life's work with you in this collection of some of his rare writings.

What Are We Negroes or Americans?

(Excerpt)

J. A. Rogers

The Messenger

Origin

Just what is a Negro? Where and how did the term originate? Is it a term of honor or reproach? These are some of the phases it is necessary to discuss.

The modern use of the term, Negro, dates back to 1442, when Antam Gonsalves, lieutenant of Prince Henry the Navigator, on a trip to the coast of Guinea brought back six captive natives from that region to Spain, a step which resulted in the African Slave Trade.

These natives were black in color, or Negro, in the Spanish or Portuguese languages, los negros (the blacks); los blancos (the whites). From Spain these negroes were taken to Cuba as slaves, and later to English-speaking America, where the word, Negro, was used, later to replace "Blackamoor" and "Ethiopian," the former English words for Black men.

The whole history of the word, Negro, except for the last sixty-one years is then associated with slavery. In other words, with things, with chattels, having no rights that "the White man was bound to respect." It is important to remember this.

Scientific Use

Later, the word with a capital "N" was to find its way

into scientific language, and acquire, perhaps, a slight measure of dignity. Johann Blumenbach (1752-1840), first of the great anthropologists, and perhaps, even at this late day, the greatest of them all, in founding the study of Man, as a science, divided the human race into five varieties, one of which he called, Negro. Blumenbach, it is important to note, was very careful to point out that his division was a purely arbitrary one, that there was, in reality, hundreds of varieties, which blended one into the other by "insensible and imperceptible" degrees; and, that when the last word had been said on the subject that there was but one race—the human race. Blumenbach did his work with the thoroughness of the German scientist, as those who will read his "Anthropological Treatise," will see.

In his book he stated in no uncertain terms his opinion that the Negro, then in the very depths of enslavement in the New World, was the biological equal of the other four varieties. And Blumenbach was in a position to know as he had a whole library filled with literary, scientific, and philosophical treatises by European Negroes, many of whom had been graduated with honors from the leading universities. The European Negro has throughout received better treatment than the African or the one in the New World. Negro slavery was abolished in Europe finally in 1773, Portugal being the last place to have Negro slaves.

Compare the thoroughness, the painstaking work, and the knowledge of the Negro as well as that of the other varieties, by this great master with that of the long line of quacks that have followed him as Madison Grant, Lothrop Stoddard, Putnam Weale, Earnest Sevier Cox, R. W. Shufeldt, Henry Fairfield Osborne, and a score of others. Verily a descent from Olympus to a mud puddle!

In Blumenbach's own words:

"Finally I am of opinion that after all these numerous instances I have brought together of Negroes of capacity, it would not be difficult to mention entire well-known provinces of Europe, from out of which you would not easily expect to obtain off hand such good authors, poets, philosophers, and correspondents of the Paris Academy; and on the other hand there is no so-called savage nation known under the sun which has so distinguished itself by such examples of perfectibility and original capacity for scientific culture, and thereby attaching itself so closely to the most civilized nations on earth, as the Negro."

Present Status

To limit now the discussion to the United States. After the Black man had been a slave for two hundred and forty-four years, during which his color and physiognomy had been so changed that within his ranks almost every type under the sun could be found, and every disgrace and ignominy known to the baseness of human nature had been heaped on him, not the least of which was the White man's religion and his doctrine of superiority, at bottom the same, he was set free to become five years later a full-fledged citizen of the United States, on the books.

There was much opposition to this, as is known, but it was nothing singular from the standpoint of ignorance and illiteracy. The bulk of the Southern Whites were in the same state that the mountaineers of Tennessee and North Carolina are now. Indeed, if the word of Olmsted, author "The Slave States," and others, is to be taken, the masses of the poor Whites were below the free Negroes and the slave domestics. The only asset of these poor Whites was the empty honor of possessing the same color, as the top dog. Hence, if these Whites could be citizens, anyone else, in common justice, could be.

Amendments To The Constitution

Citizenship and suffrage, as it ought to be well-known, were conferred by the Fourteenth and Fifteenth Amendments to the Constitution. Since it is certain that comparatively few Negroes have read them, it is well to quote them here:

Art. XIV says in part: "All persons, born or naturalized in the United States and subject to the jurisdiction thereof, are citizens of the United States, and of the States wherein they reside. No State shall make or enforce any law which shall abridge the privileges or immunities of citizens of the United States."

Art. XV. "The right of citizens of the United States shall not be denied or abridged by the United States or by any State on account of color, race, or previous condition of servitude."

When Is A Negro A Negro?

As the term, Negro, stands today it is fully as undefinable as electricity. A white-skinned person who is legally a White man in North Carolina can be legally a Negro in the adjoining state of Virginia; one legally White in Virginia will be classed as Black in Oklahoma; the same person legally White in Oregon will be legally Black in North Carolina; the whole definition for America being as uncertain and crotchety as an old maid. Each state acts according to its prejudices, or clearer yet, the exploitable possibilities of the "Negro."

Many contend that the term, Negro, is one of opprobrium. There can be no doubt that it is. It was founded on slavery and forced degradation. Further, in many of the Southern

States, as in South Carolina, Louisiana, and Georgia and those states, in which the population is so mixed that the imputation is likely to be true it is as libelous to call one, supposedly White, a Negro, as to call him a horse-thief, pimp, or crap-shooter. Some years ago a newspaper in South Carolina, in reporting a story, accidentally called a supposedly White man, Colored. The judge in awarding him damages uttered this remarkable bit of legal wisdom: "...if one race be inferior to the other socially the Constitution of the United States cannot put them on the same plane." In North Carolina a man recently brought suit when called Negro.

At the mere mention of the word, Negro, particularly in White newspapers, fully ninety percent of the population of the United States, regardless of color, experience a feeling of repulsion, except in certain instances, such as when it comes to telling what the "Negro" has done for the country. Hence the just contention of those who insist the term is a debasing one. As to the word, nigger, there is really no difference, except that custom has made it so. Apart from the fact that the majority of "Negroes" refer to themselves as "niggers," that word, is only the slip-shod pronunciation, as "sah," for "sir." It is certain that the perverters of the word had no added insult in mind.

The objectors to the word, Negro, as was said, are right, but when they suggest some other word as "Colored," Ethiopian, Ethican, Afro-American, Race-man, they but constitute themselves killers of time, and diverters from the main issue, the getting of one's rights. For it is not the name but the treatment that hurts. Anglo-Saxon, Christian, Yankee, Irish, and a host of other names were once terms of reproach. When the social, that is, the economic standing of the possessors of those names had improved, the terms also acquired dignity. With loss of economic standing names also lose their standing as Greek, Spaniard, Turk, Italian. Call the Black man White, and the

White man Black; reverse the terms Negro and Caucasian, and with treatment unchanged it will make no difference.

And the worst part of it is that the proscribed is bound to use, some time or another, the opprobrious name, given by the oppressor. For instance, in the South the "Negro" is forced by law into separate places labeled for him. In describing himself in legal documents in every state in the Union, and seen in the departments conducted by the United States Government itself he is compelled to describe himself as "Negro" or "Colored," as in marriage license, criminal proceedings, naturalization proceedings, Federal positions, census reports. Although the Constitution of the Federal Government, itself, declare that he is a citizen, yet the government goes to the length of denying this by writing him down as "Colored" or "Negro" in the census reports. It is noteworthy, in this respect that it is only those incapable of becoming citizens, who are thus enumerated separately, as Indians, Chinese, Japanese. Those of other nationalities as, Italians, Jews, Greeks, Germans, provided they are native-born are never mentioned as such. If not born here they are all classified as foreign-born Whites. In short, though the Federal government calls the so-called Negro, a citizen, it classifies him as an alien, or rather something betwixt and between, that something, as I will later show being still a slave, to a certain degree of the White man.

Because this is so the Supreme Court of the United States, final voice of the Federal Government, always with an eye to the preservation of property rights has been notorious in its decisions as to what is justice for the Black man—an old story dating from the Dred Scott decision to the present segregation affair in Washington, D. C.

Although forbidden by the Constitution to make or enforce any bill based on color, these injunctions, to every state south of the Mason-Dixon Line and some north of it are but so many scraps of paper. "Negroes" are forced to pay the same taxes, the same railroad fare, poll-tax, bound to the same contracts, in short the same civic obligations as the White man. But when it comes to getting returns for his harder-earned dollar he gets less, anywhere from seventy-five to twenty cents, and in the matter of education sometimes as low as five cents to the dollar.

On a recent trip to the South I rode from Wilmington, N. C., to Richmond on an old wooden Jim Crow car placed between a modern steel baggage car, and steel coach for Whites. In a collision the Colored coach, if one can dignify it by that name, would have been crushed to tinder. Further, the conductor, the railroad employees, and the news "butcher" pre-empted eight places while passengers stood. The toilet room of the Colored women happened to be nearest the baggage car, so the employees on that car, used it. Further the Colored car is always placed ahead, so that in case of a head-on collision, the "Negroes" will get killed first. This by the way, is about the only instance in the South where the Black man goes first, in jim–crow street cars he rides in the rear. Yet there is an impartial fare for both. This, of course, is only a very minor incident. This article is pianissimo.

In all of these Jim Crow states a Negro may ride in the White coach provided he is in the employ of some White person or is a prisoner. Hence, if all Negroes travelled as servants or as convicts, there would be no Jim Crow cars.

Sufficient has been said in answer to the query at the head of this article to prove that in actuality, and regardless of what the Constitution may say we are not Americans, but "Negroes" or "Colored" as the census reports define us. By and large we have not even the rights of the alien, even those aliens incapable of becoming citizens. With my own ears I heard the terrific fight put up, by ministers of the gospel in Virginia senate last February to keep Chinese, Japanese, and other Asiatics from being Jim Crowed in conveyances and public places, and they won. A so-called race integrity bill which passed the house ingeniously declared that the bill would not affect those persons "who by the Constitution of the United States are ineligible to become citizens of the United States," meaning Asiatics. Think of that! Chinese, Japanese, and Mexicans ride where they please in the South.

Then there is the Indian, a ward of the nation, and living on the reservation. He pays no taxes but when he comes among the Whites, with the saloons now illegal, he may go where he pleases. No segregation for him. The same holds true of any European who touches these shores. There is no segregation for a German, though he made a thousand American widows in the last war. There is segregation for the "Negro" veteran, though he saved a thousand from becoming widows, unless he is travelling as valet for the German.

The sole purpose of segregation is to preserve the status of slave and master—to so arrange it that the "Negro" will have a back-door entrance to everything.

Nor, as was said, is the Federal Government any stricter in the enforcement of the law than the states. Washington, D. C. is under the direct rule of the President and Congress, yet but for the Jim Crow car one might well be in Mississippi.

But after all the Negro has been taught on the subject of citizenship, the above will sound incredible. Am I at no time a citizen, he will ask. Yes, there are times when he is not only a citizen, but he is compelled to be, and this holds true of the most barbarous of the Cracker states as of the Northern ones. When it comes to paying taxes, to service in the draft, to defense of the country as in case of foreign invasion, in short in all those things that make for the White man's benefit, he is a one hundred percent citizen. In those that makes for his own benefit, he is only a Negro. In things that make for the White man's benefit the United States is to the Negro, a nation; in things that make for his own benefit, it is a race or tribe, and he an alien in it...

VIRGINIA WARS ON "INTEGRITY" BILL

HAMPTON IS CENTER OF HOT FIGHT

"Blue Bloods" Liven Up Hearing In Legislature As Unnatural Shades Of Color and Social Equality Are Attacked.

The Pittsburgh Courier
February 27, 1926
J. A. Rogers
(Special to The Pittsburgh Courier)

RICHMOND, Va., Feb. 25—Those who have never been south of the Mason-Dixon Line may think they know something about the real color struggle, but it is my firm conviction that they don't. I say this after hearing the arguments on the so-called race integrity bill which came up recently for a hearing before a committee in the Virginia senate. So-called Negroes who have always lived in the North can have no idea what their Southern brethren are really up against. And Virginia is highly civilized, compared with Mississippi. In those three hours I learned more about the psychology of the Southern White than I have in three years.

At a similar hearing in any Northern legislature, except perhaps states like Indiana, the issue would be whether there should be segregation. At that hearing segregation was taken as a prime necessity by both attackers and advocates of the bill. As I heard both sides vaunting of White Supremacy and of the magic qualities supposed to inhere in the purity of Anglo-Saxon blood—God only knows what that is—I really couldn't decide which side I objected to the more. If anything my sympathies were with the advocates for they at least were frank, while the attackers attempted to pacify and smooth over, and really seemed alarmed over the Chinese and the Japanese, that one would have thought they were the citizens and the Negro the alien. Well, the Japanese have battleships, and the Colored folk, well…

Hampton Institute

The fight centered around Hampton Institute, which seems to be a little too prosperous to jive with current notions of "White superiority." Later when stirring editorials from the Crisis and the Norfolk Journal and Guide were blocked by the opposition, and I noted how the assembled solons were about to stampede by the little they had heard of them, then I realized what the opposers of the bill were up against. They had their head in the lion's mouth and were trying to ease it out. This is why I say that the Northern Negro doesn't know what the Southern one is up against. The average White Northerner is an angel of reasonableness compared with the Southerner.

Hampton was accused of the "horrible practice of social equality." Delegate Massenburge, who led the attack, began with the usual bunk about the love for Colored folk and that he "couldn't see where Colored people could be offended by segregation laws." He painted a horrible picture of the conditions said to exist at Hampton and the fearful results that would follow if not checked—said horrible condition being that citizens of different colors sat side by side in a theatre there.

The next speaker was Col. W. S. Copeland, a tall, lanky, typical-looking Southerner, who talked in short jerks with his mouth almost closed. Please don't ask me what brigade the colonel commanded in the last war or any war.

The colonel, who is a publisher of the Newport News Daily News, showed that he was a good Anglo-Saxon by the way he murdered the King's English, also vehemently pretested how fond he was of Colored folk. Indeed, everyone, friend and foe, was telling so much how he loved us that I had great difficulty in restraining myself from shedding a few crocodile tears, too.

The colonel who told the usual story about his people having owned slaves, his Black mammy, and so on, said:

"The Niggers in that institution IS being taught that there ought not to be any distinction between themselves and White people. If you wipe out the color line we are gone. There will be no power on earth to prevent the Nigger from entering our homes and marrying your daughter. We are going to have serious trouble if you do not pass this act to protect our citizens and our womanhood against this horrible practice of social equality."

Using the Dennishawn Players, who danced at Hampton Institute, as a horrible example the colonel raved:

"There they were beautiful White women in the nude with Nigger youths gazing at them, and there was the flower of our womanhood seated next to the Black. There are a certain amount of our women who cannot resist temptation and it is our duty to protect them by maintaining the barrier that southern manhood has always stood for."

Attacks N.A.A.C.P. and Journal and Guide

John Powell, founder of the Anglo-Saxon Clubs, speaking in favor of the bill began by praising "the Negroes of Virginia for not pressing against the color line." He bitterly attacked the N.A.A.C.P., those who were responsible for the chorus of Colored women which recently refused to sing in Washington,

D.C., as well as those who attacked Roland Hayes for singing before a segregated audience. "I warn you, gentlemen," he said, "that Virginia, which has maintained the color line for three hundred years, has been chosen for attack because of its well-known leniency. The Norfolk Journal and Guide, one of the most powerful organs of opinion among Negroes is making this breaking down of the color line a matter of principle. Nothing could be more incendiary than to oppose this bill."

Unnatural Shades of Color

Rev. Dr. Love, White, in opposing the bill, took a slap at persons of mixed ancestry. This man of God, who, perhaps, preaches that God made us all, spoke of the "unnatural shades of color due to race mixing." He declared that he was in favor of segregation and Anglo-Saxon ideals, but said that the proposed bill was unjust because it would impose a law upon the whole state in order to correct a condition said to exist at Hampton.

The bill, he further said, threw "an unwarranted reflection on the White race, the presumption being raised by the bill is that all over Virginia the White people must be restrained by law from promiscuous mingling and association with Negroes." The reverend gentleman seemed especially exercised over the fact that Chinese, Japanese and other Colored aliens, not now affected by the present Jim Crow laws, which he favors for Negroes, would be included in the bill.

The bill, which requires "the separation of White and Colored persons at public halls…public assemblages, etc.," includes all non-White persons. This, he said, "includes the chapels at the University of Richmond, Union Theological Seminary and other like institutions. This is an application of race agitation with a vengeance. The churches are fighting hard to keep the Chinese and Japanese from being included. Think what it would mean to our missionaries in the East. This document made into law would put Chinese students and gentlemen who come to Richmond to patronize commercial houses and buy tobacco in Jim Crow cars."

The reverend gentleman said a mouthful when he began to play on the pocketbook nerve. The seminaries referred to might also find a shrinkage of income should foreign students be frightened away. But fancy asking a law against a group of citizens which the state is afraid to apply to aliens! Such a thing could happen nowhere else, but in America. Still later we might be called upon to be loyal in a struggle with Japan.

Bitterly opposed as I am to segregation for once I find myself in favor of this bill: If passed it would probably increase the Colored population in this state to the point, where it far exceeded the White. Many of the most influential Virginians who now despise Negroes, as well as mixed Indians would be included. Personally, I fail to see how the bill could further humiliate Negroes. As to Hampton Institute I understand the passage of the bill would affect the Whites most, as it would mean the closing of Ogden Hall, where they have been attending shows at about a quarter of the ordinary price.

But, as I said, I suppose the Japanese will be excluded because they have a government and battleships, however, in the frantic attempt to keep them out of the Jim Crow car is the best proof that riding there is considered a disadvantage and an insult.

Members of the legislature, who, as was said, got quite panicky when they read Du Bois' editorial as to what Dr. Gregg should have answered, clamored for Dr. Gregg, who was absent, and wanted to know whether there were any "100 percent Virginians" (White, of course) on the faculty at Hampton.

Social Equality

Rev. W. T. Johnson of the First Baptist Church made a soothing diplomatic speech, saying that he loved the White race. He said: "I regard your race as mine for I love you and you love me." He went on to tell of the cordial relations that exist in our beloved state of Virginia, "how the Negro had served loyally in the war and how the proposed legislation would bring discouragement, uneasiness and discomfort." He further denied that the Negro wanted social equality. It was only justice, he asked.

Things are either equal or unequal, and if the Negro does not want social equality, what does he wish, social inequality? It is a common sight here to see a Negro chauffeur seated besides the wife or daughter of his White employer, but let that same chauffeur take a seat in a car or theatre, beside the lowest class person who happened to be White and that is construed as social equality. Dr. Gregg was denounced by someone for favoring social equality, because it is said that Dr. Gregg advocated Colored men on juries. If social equality is good for one set of Americans, it is good for all. As to social recognition, that is for the individual to decide.

To Correct Situation

One of the trustees of Hampton, whose name I did not bear, but later learned was Homer D. Ferguson, said:

"One interesting fact is that we are all in favor of segregation…the situation at Hampton will be corrected or we Southern White men will get off the board. The students are taught not to mix with the White race, but Northern teachers make it difficult." The gallery was full of White people, but the only Colored one present besides Dr. Johnson were visitors from the city, Mr. Louis G. Gregory, the Baha'ist lecturer, and myself. We too had a rather interesting experience. A White man, three parts drunk, came over to where we were sitting. He waxed quite confidently telling us that he had served eight years in the legislature, told us of the sex relations he had had with his mother's Colored maid. When I asked him whether he was in favor of segregation, he replied no because he said its only purpose was the exploitation of the Negro, economically and sexually.

Next week I will tell of my interview with Messrs. Cox and Powell and my impressions of them.

TO COMPILE RECORD OF RACE NOTABLES

J. A. ROGERS GETS "FIRST HAND" IMPRESSION OF "BLUE BLOOD" BOOSTERS

Says Interview With Powell and Cox Made Him Feel As Though He Were In Presence Of the Devil—Classifies Them As Sincere, But Dangerous.

AMAZING REVELATION TO BE MADE NEXT WEEK

The Pittsburgh Courier
March 6, 1926
J. A. Rogers
(Special to The Pittsburgh Courier)

RICHMOND, Va., Mar. 4—"I'm glad you did not find us the ogres we're said to be," said John Powell, founder of the Anglo-Saxon Clubs in parting after our third meeting. "Now," he added, kindly, "if we can do anything for you be sure to let us know."

And truth to say I had not. Quite otherwise. I had found him and his co-worker, Earnest Sevier Cox, to be very fine gentlemen, indeed. Powell is earnest, sympathetic, and very kindly; Cox is jovial, mild mannered, and quite likeable. He has travelled much, particularly in Africa, and has the free and easy manner of the globe-trotter. Had I never heard of the kind of propaganda they are engaged in I felt I could have liked them just as much as some of my excellent friends, Colored or White. Both men showed, moreover, an extreme solicitude at present Negro injustices. Both seemed much moved when I told of the slaughter in the Chicago riot.

BUT—

It is just here that appearances are most deceptive; it is here where so many Colored folk permit themselves to be deceived for it is from just such affable sources flow the agitation which culminate in lynchings, race riot and racial discords, which is the bane in this economic paradise of America. As I listened to them my mind flew back to horrible scenes of butchery I witnessed in the Chicago riot, fomented by such pleasant gentlemen as these and I felt, indeed, as I were having an interview with the Devil, himself.

Powell, particularly, strikes me as being sincere. But who knows but that the Devil is quite sincere in his mischief. There are doctrines, the preaching of which stir strife, bloodshed and war; there are also doctrines which spread love and light and healing. Who doubts that an apostle of the former can be quite as sincere as the latter? If there is a Devil, you may wager, you may depend upon it, he is quite an affable fellow: it is his imps who are the coarse fellows, and in this case it is the rag-tags and bobtails—the lynchers—who are the uncouth ones, and not those at the fountain head of mischief, like Messrs. Cox, Plecker and Powell.

It has been charged that both men are agitating chiefly for personal gain. Powell, it is rumored, is peeved, because it is said that Nathaniel Dett was chosen over him in a piano recital—but I don't think so. Both are suffering, in my opinion, particularly Powell, from swollen ego. Had they grown up in a country where there were no Negroes their excessive conceit would have found expression in dislike for members of their own so-called race. They would have been good haters of the English, French, Germans, Americans, as the case may be. Their anti-Negro feeling is only incidental.

Indeed, there ought to be nothing remarkable about this type to us, so-called Negroes, for have we not our ultra-racialists? Change the color of men like the three above mentioned—sacrilegious thought—to black, yellow, or brown, and they would bark as loudly on the other side of the fence as they are now doing on this. It is not a matter of race, but of human nature—the nature of the man who is not happy unless he is maintaining a caste or looking down upon a fellow-man.

Garvey Enthusiasts

Both are intensely interested in Garvey and are hacking his movement. Powell says that Garvey is one of the greatest influences that has ever come into his life and anxiously asked me whether I thought him guilty. I replied that to the best of my knowledge he had not been guilty of theft, but that false representations had undoubtedly been made to promote the sale of stock and that the law had held him, as head of the Black Star Line, responsible. Both declared that his imprisonment was a great injustice, and wanted to know if there was such a thing as justice on this earth.

After discussing the matter of Garvey's proposed release and deportation we came to the African colonization plan, which both are trying to push hard through the present session of the legislature, and which they say intend to try to have introduced in all the legislatures and Congress.

"The White man," said Cox, "tore your people from Africa, robbed you of all your land and your tribal rights. He crowded you in vile ships and brought you to these shores. But he may now furnish you with ships and every comfort to take you back. We intend to see that this nation acquire African territory and divide the land among you as our government acquired the West. We pledge the White man to use his ships to carry you home, his weapons to fight your enemies, and his implements of peace to make you a wealthy people."

I thought this even fishier than the famous promise of "forty acres and a mule," and suggested that the European powers had Africa pretty well sewed up, especially so far as the American Negro was concerned. The latter, I said, was feared throughout the length and breadth of Africa because of his democratic ideals and I mentioned the complications I brought down on myself when I innocently asked for a vise to go to Africa. I said that the sole hope was the break-up of European domination, but Cox didn't seem to enjoy that.

"There is Liberia," replied Cox. "Liberia is capable of holding all the Negroes in America. Your only hope is colonization, for as long as the Negro remains here he will be exploited. The Chamber of Commerce wants the Negro here because they want to rob him. It is a shame."

"We stand for absolute equality of justice for both races," said Powell, "but they must be separate. Segregation which has lasted three hundred years in this state, must not be broken down. Race mixing is biologically bad."

Now I am a mixed blood and don't think I'm such a bad fellow at that, so I thought he wasn't quite complimentary. Ignoring this, however, I again suggested that from what I had learnt of the psychology of the Americo-Liberian I was led to believe that any large number of American Negroes there would be as little welcome as on British soil. I pointed out, also, that the growth of any given population was the result of evolution, and that in the shifting of a large number of population we'd have two problems instead of one on our hands—one in the place from which it was shifted and another where it was taken. However, it strikes me that deportation is one easy way to settle the Hampton Institute situation and that if these gentlemen have their way I will be able to visit Africa after all.

Cox wanted to know whether Negroes would be willing to go "back" to Africa. I told him that I knew a few who were very eager to do so, but that the majority were such good Americans that when any of the number got disgusted and went to France or South America, they, like the yellow cat, promptly came back.

"Tell me," flashed Powell, "have your people no pride!" Their theory is that the Negro who wants to stay here lacks pride. Cox says: "Were I commissioned to retain a part of your race in America and send the others away I would retain those who wish to go and send those who wish to remain. If I kept any it would be those who wish to build a nation of your won. If my race must lose its purity, pray God that the aliens who enter be those who value their own blood and seek to express its worth." This statement, by the way, shows that he regards amalgamation as inevitable unless the Negro is taken deported.

Powell's question was timely. It made me wonder in face of present treatment how the governments of the several states and even the federal government itself would take it if Negroes so-called showed more manly pride. One thing I felt sure that professional White men like these wouldn't find such easy sledding.

I replied to the effect that the entire training of the so-called Negro was to make him an American citizen just as the White child. That gods, heroes, and flags of both were the same; that in the matter of paying taxes and national duty such as service in time of war the so-called Negro is such a full-fledged citizen; in short, that in all those things that made for the White man's benefit the Negro was an American, but that in those things that made for his own benefit he was only a Negro.

"You and other White men," I said to Cox, two days later, "have a perfect right to keep yourselves to yourselves, and to agitate for same. You all have a right to think yourselves superior to Negroes, but no right to treat them unjustly. The Negro has at least a hard time earning his dollar as has the White man. Under segregation, however, as exists in the South, the Negro gets less for his dollar than the White man. Who gets what the Negro has lost? Segregation laws are designed expressly for the benefit of their makers."

Both men declared that they stand absolutely for equal justice to both "races" and are working hard to bring it about.

The thing I had been eagerly waiting to hear finally came up for a discussion. I wanted to know how they re-acted to the fact brought out by the discussion of the so-called race integrity bill that some twenty thousand of the leading families of Virginia were Colored.

Cox brought it up, treating the whole thing as a very good joke. "What do you think of our little comedy in the legislature?" he asked laughingly. To Powell, the zealot, it was no laughing matter, however. Cox went on to tell how very mixed with Negro were some of the Indians, whom the legislature in view of the recent disclosures, wanted to class as White. These mixed Indians, he said, had the highest contempt for Negroes, who in turn disliked them.

"Stop off at West Point," they said, "and ask any Negro there what he thinks of those Indians."

Both say they are working hard to make illicit sex relations between the so-called races a crime, but that the legislators didn't seem so keen for that bill. Powell, I also learnt, has been spreading his propaganda through all the Southern legislatures, where he has given addresses. Both men are also hard at work, fostering Jim Crow legislation in Northern states, particularly Ohio. They bear the inter-racialists, the N.A.A.C.P., and the Negro press no particular goodwill.

VIRGINIA'S 'RACE INTEGRITY' WAR ATTRACTING ENTIRE NATION

J. A. Rogers Tells How White Papers are Capitalizing on Fight Of "First Families"

Sensational Headlines and News Articles Tell Of Many Instances Of Race Mixing—Thousands Of People Involved, Alleged.

The Pittsburgh Courier
March 13, 1926
J. A. Rogers

We Colored folk, have long insisted that the so-called Anglo-Saxon in the South carriers so much of our blood in his veins that if "the color line" were accurately drawn we'd be the dominant group over-night. I venture to say that there is not a single one of the ten or twelve millions of us, declared Negroes, who does not know at least one "Negro" who can "pass" in any company of blondes, and at least one who is "passing."—I know scores. Since this is so, it means that we are hundreds of thousands, perhaps, millions of others who are of Negro ancestry and never dream it.

Our individual experiences in this matter would make a most astonishing volume, indeed.

But we haven't it recorded in black and white, which is what counts. There are "The Beginnings of Miscegenation," by Carter G. Woodson; "The Social History of the American Family," by Calhoun, a White man, and other books to prove that the Whites, from the highest to the lowest, have been mixing to a greater or less degree with Negroes since the first recorded instance in 1630 in Hening's Statutes of Virginia.

It is also well-known that the Indian and the Negro mixed freely from the beginning, and that in later years, the Indian has carried through legalized marriage a tremendous amount of Negro strain into the White. Indeed, the so-called Anglo-Saxon in the South is so mixed that it would be as impossible to tell who is "White" and who is not as it would be to pick out the white meat from the dark in a bowl of finely-ground chicken hash.

But now, thanks to what I regard as the most amazing expose' of race mixing I have ever seen, we may speak of present day conditions, not as the priests and scribes, but with authority. I, myself, have made some studies in race-mixing, past and present, in "As Nature Leads," and had ransacked libraries and questioned individuals for such matter without getting it nearly as fully, and as authoritatively. In their frantic endeavor to maintain exploiting an aristocracy based on complexion and to overcome the lure of black—that is in the other fellow, Virginians have, in Richmond, a fire-proof building in which is being kept a record of everyone according to "race," known as the Bureau of Vital Statistics. I had been planning to go into this building to do a little "digging" when to my intense good fortune I found that John Powell, founder of the Anglo-Saxon Clubs, who is waging a stern and bitter fight to weed out the goats from the sheep, had saved me the trouble, and was publishing the facts in a series of articles in the Richmond Times-Despatch. Powell, who is much hated by those Whites, who are not so anxious to have their ancestry looked into, also appears to be backed up in his information by two professors, one from Goucher College, Baltimore, who have been conducting investigations under the auspices of the Carnegie Institute and are to publish soon a book called "Mongrel Virginians."

It is safe to say that no Negro sociologist could have had such findings published in a White newspaper, and I can account for the publication of them after hot protest, only on the ground that agitation for ”race integrity” has brought a circulation to the papers equaled only by war time. One paper that carried the head: 64 ARISTOCRATIC VA. FAMILIES Colored, sold like hot cakes. Not less than twenty thousand of the leading families have been found to be Colored. Persons who have never been South can have no idea what a tremendous social and economic loss it would mean to these families if forced across the line. For instance, at the time of writing, Negroes in Norfolk are barred from an art exhibit in which Tanner's pictures are being shown. A special day is to be set apart for them, it is said.

The Last Stand

There are twelve articles in all, covering the ten Congressional districts. They deal only with Virginia, but they depict conditions which are typical of the South, particularly states like South Carolina, Georgia and Mississippi, and furnish such splendid proof that race purity is a myth that it is a pity they couldn't be published entire. I shall endeavor to give a digest of them, however, they bear the significant title "The Last Stand." It will be noticed, from time to time that Powell makes desperate apologies as if he fears he were lifting the veil a little too much.

After a brief review of the attempt alleged to have been made by Virginia to bar Negro slavery, the African Colonization movements, the ousting of the carpet-bagger, and the re-establishment of White Supremacy, the writer goes on:

"But this battle had been fought and won in the political field. The most immediate, the most pressing dangers had been political. The more remote but graver threat was forgotten or ignored. In re-establishing and confirming White Supremacy our people lost sight of, and neglected racial integrity. The necessity for rebuilding prosperity from devastation absorbed attention. Slaves, which had furthered the mongrelization of the Negro race, had effectively protected the Whites from blood admixture. Under the new order the protection no longer existed. Near-White mix-breeds, no longer the property of masters, could attain positions of relative independence, and remove freely to localities where their racial antecedents were unknown. The anti-miscegenation laws were defective; while loudly proclaiming the axiom that one drop of Negro blood makes the Negro, the Whites defined a Negro by statute as an individual possessing one-fourth or more African blood, later as an individual with one-eighth or more African blood, and still later with one-sixteenth or more. Under these defective laws many mix-breeds actually went into court, had themselves declared legally White, and married White persons.

Instances of Race-Mixing

"Case No. 1. Accomac County."
(On file in the State Records.)

"A White woman of Accomac County married an immigrant from one of the Southern States, whose antecedents were unknown to her. Doubts having arisen as to his racial purity, inquiries were instituted which discovered that his birth-record in his native State showed him to be a Negro. Two grandchildren of this union have written to the Virginia Bureau of Vital Statistics asking for evidence to prove that they are White. One wrote from Northampton County, the other from a Northern State. This case is a terrifying example with which mixed blood can become dispersed over wide geographical areas. Many similar instances are reported by the clerks of various county courts.

"Case No. 2. Essex County."
(Birth record in county files.)

"A young mix-breed of pleasing manner and appearance came from Essex County to enter business in a city in another district. He met and eventually married into a wealthy family. Recently, friends of the young wife learnt that her husband was entered in the Essex records as a Negro..."

Indian Chief Proves To Be Negro

Cases 3 and 4 deal with a child of mixed White, Negro and Indian who passed for White, and with a Negro from Caroline, Va., who "married a White woman of a good family," irrespectively. Case No. 5, also on file, deals with a group of Indians who had been marrying with Whites, "claiming a semi-miraculous origin from two pure-blood Indian maidens discovered, dryad-like, in a hollow tree by an Englishman, who married one of them...records prove the presence of Negro blood in this group...the marriage records of the grandparents of one of the chiefs bears on it the annotation, free Negro."

Of case No. 6, "On file in the State records," the writer says:

"This case is important in that it shows not only the actual process of amalgamation, but exhibits the most appalling instance of the decay of decency and race pride which constitutes the psychological basis of the color line. It is inexpressibly humiliating to bring such an affair to notice, but if we are to gain a true concept of conditions as they exist, it is necessary to look facts in the face. Only so, can we cope with the situation. The facts will be presented with as much reticence as possible." This case is that of a White woman who left her husband and returned to him two years later with a Mulatto child. He took her back.

"Other children were born to her, some White, some Colored, her husband apparently making no protest...The complaisance of the White father is perhaps the most revolting feature of the story."

Powell gives many instances of apparently White couples bearing Black children. It seems that the above story can explain all.

The writer continues: "Material similar to these six cases could be deduced from practically every county of the First District. In the files of the Bureau of Vital Statistics, alone, are instances from six of the sixteen counties, and this, too, notwithstanding that the bureau has only been working intensively in this field since June, 1924, and has no means at its disposal wherewith to undertake investigations on its own initiative."

Verily, it seems as if the stable is being locked after the horse has escaped.

Indians Proven Negroes

The cases in the Second and Third Districts deal with groups of Negro-hating Indians of Negro and White ancestry, who went through a "fry-fish ceremony" to prove they were Indians. "The fish were fried and eaten. Sacramental and transmutative fish. Before eating, Negroes; after eating, Indians." Other cases are that of a "light" Negro, who married a White girl; of a group of mixed Indian, White and Negro "families" of which "have removed to Norfolk and Portsmouth and intermarried with White people;" of a family, which registered its eight children as now White, now Colored;" while the racial status of the last child, born 1924, is recorded with a question mark; of two White sisters, who married a Negro and a Chinaman.

Marries Into Prominent White Family

Among those in the Fourth District are those of a Negro, who "moved over into Chesterfield and married into a White family of prominence in this county, where he and his wife are now living; of a woman who was married "into a prominent family." After her children were grown, it was discovered by chance that she was recorded in her native state as a Negro; of a White woman, who had "one White and two Colored" children; of "a well-dressed, well-mannered and evidently prosperous woman," who came "to establish her claims to aristocratic descent" and "discovered that she was descended from Negroes;" of "a wealthy farmer," married "to a woman of refinement and culture," who lost his mother a few years ago. The neighbors came to the funeral. There appeared also Negroes, claiming to be his brothers and sisters. They were apparently received as such. "These Negroes are illegitimate children born to my mother, after my father's death."

"It is impossible, " adds Powell, "to conceive anything more appalling than this case, or more indicative of the precarious condition of the color line."

Negro Girl Reared in Luxury

The Fifth District tells among other cases of a group which has been marrying among its White neighbors, claiming that its members are "Cuban Indians" although "the United States Ethnological Bureau states that they are mixed White and Indian with a considerable infusion of Negro;" of "mixed breed children of a White mother who were entered in the high school;" of several groups of Whites and Negroes who live in illicit relations in Halifax County, their offspring going to other parts and "passing;" and of "a member of a wealthy family which even the War of Secession could not impoverish, who remained as a bachelor living at his county seat. His Negro housekeeper bore him a daughter, around whom he centered all his affection and paternal instinct." This girl, it is said, received the best that money could buy, and was married to a Negro. The wedding cake was baked by her father's White sister-in-law.

In this same district the following remarkable case is noted as follows:

"An Appalling Situation."
"Case No. IX. X County"
(Reported to the Bureau of Vital Statistics).

"The facts now to be presented set forth the most ghastly and appalling conditions existent within the State. To spare the sensibilities of the White inhabitants, it is deemed best not to disclose the name of the county. A judge from another district was recently holding court in X County. The wife of a White man who was a party in one of the cases was pointed out to the judge. She was obviously Negroid. When the court adjourned the judge asked the clerk of the court for an explanation of this situation. The clerk replied that the man was White and that the wife was Negroid. The judge asked if the clerk had issued the license for the marriage. The clerk replied in the affirmative, explaining that the family of the wife, although undoubtedly Negroid, had been passing for White for several generations, and was of sufficient influence to make refusal to grant the license out of the question. He added that this case was not unique in X County, but was typical of a widespread condition. The judge took the first opportunity to visit the Bureau of Vital Statistics and report the matter. On arriving at the office he found, by strange coincidence, a minister of the gospel from X County, who had come to report what he knew of conditions there. At first he had been reticent as to names and places, but encouraged by the judge he finally became more communicative and gave the names of several men whom he thought would be frank and courageous enough to give specific information. The State registrar wrote these men; only one dared reply. He sent in several pages filled with such information as the following:

"Richard Doe, mixed; wife, White."
"The Z family, mixed, pass for White and have married with Whites."
Etc., etc.....

"The pure Whites of this county are afraid openly to expose the situation or to take any steps to control it, so numerous and influential are the mixed breeds, and so widely connected by marriage. A member of the House of Delegates and a State Senator were recently discussing the situation in this county. 'I estimate that at least one-third of the White population of X County are more or less Negroid.' The Senator replied: You put it too low, I should say at least one-half."

The other districts with perhaps even more striking cases will be given next week, as well as the types of the 64 aristocrats who are said to be Colored, among which, it is claimed, are two presidents of the United States.

J. A. ROGERS REVEALS FURTHER MIXING OF RACES IN VIRGINIA

Says He Would Probably Be Lynched In Some Parts Of Country For Articles

---

Powell Continues Tirade Against Interbreeding Of Races As Rogers Lets "Cat Out Of Bag"—Tells How Slave Married White Woman and Other Sensational Cases

---

The Pittsburgh Courier
March 20, 1926
J. A. Rogers

RICHMOND, Va., March 18—In my last article I pointed out that there is much opposition to the so-called race integrity bill because it took in "too much territory." The state would have had quite a job increasing its Jim Crow accommodations, or rather lack of accommodation. Among the number that would be classed as Colored according to the Richmond News-Leader (White), February 9, would be: "Two United States Senators, a United States ambassador to France, two secretaries of war, two presidents of the United States, five generals, three of the most distinguished of living Southern novelists, three governors of Virginia, a speaker of the House of Representatives, two bishops, three congressmen, one rear-admiral, two judges of the Virginia supreme court, and many of the foremost officers of the Confederate Army." Some of these are dead but many have no doubt left families.

The bill as passed by the House has been considerably modified. One interesting feature of it is the adroit wording by which Asiatics are not affected but native and foreign-born

Negroes are. It "is not applicable to non-White foreign persons who are ineligible to citizenship in this country." That is, if you can't become a citizen of the United States you are O.K.

The Last Stand

To continue my review of the revelations of race-mixing culled from official documents by John Powell, the dark-skinned Nordic agitator for a 101 percent lily-white. The article, if published by a Negro in parts of the South, would probably have brought the mob at his heels.

Speaking of Montgomery County, Powell writes:

"In this county there is a considerable group of near-white mix-breeds, who are beginning to spread out into other communities. Although they vigorously assert their claim to a White status, the White people have never allowed it. It would be almost impossible to have them correctly recorded in the vital statistics of the State. The local registrars would meet with serious violence were they to record them as other than White. A leading citizen of Blacksburg stated that it would be necessary to take a company of troops into the section were an attempt made to record them properly."

Case No. 2 is of a group of mixed Indian, White and Negro "descended from slaves who had removed from their native localities," who call themselves Indians. Some of these people in neighboring counties "succeed in passing" and in "marrying Whites." A county official says: "I list them as Colored people but it makes them mad to be so listed. I know they are not White, and I know that some of them have married into White families."

Another case tells of a man who "claimed that he was

White, but the claim was never allowed," who cohabitated with several White women of the neighborhood other than his wife, having several children, who "make no such claim, associate with the Negroes, and several of them have married Negroes."

Case 3 is of "a White woman, the mother of five children and living with a husband, who was indubitably White, gave birth to a Mulatto child. As the husband apparently accepted the child as his own the mid-wife could not do otherwise than to make out the White birth certificate. She objected, however, to the director of the city bureau, who in his report to the state registrar says: "I hesitate to change the birth certificate, but several weeks ago Mrs. X—was convicted of unlawful habitation with a Negro and plead guilty—"

Yet after giving many instances as these the writer continues to speak of reversion, which by the way, if true, would score one for Negro strain. If one "drop" of "Negro blood" could knock out 99 of "White blood," would it not show the extraordinary strength of the former. And since when does strength become something to be ashamed of?

Slave and a White Woman.

In another congressional district is the case of a slave who shortly before the Civil War ran away with a White woman, "who afterwards bore Mulatto twins, both female. Owing to their White maternity, the twins passed for White and both married White men." From these unions have sprung two large groups, the R—s and the N—s. There are also White R—s and N—s in the county but it almost passes human ingenuity to distinguish the White R—s and N—s from the mixed R—s and N—s.

Other cases deal with White women who have presented their husbands with Colored children; another who had several White children and one Colored, of which the butler is believed to be the father.

Thrown in Hog-Pen

This case in another district is interesting. "Case No. 1 Loudon County (on file in the State records):

A near White baby was born to a Negro servant and was placed by the mother in the pig-pen to be devoured by the pigs. The employer of the servant discovered the baby and rescued it. It was a girl. The child was adopted by a childless White couple, is now twenty years old, has blue eyes and fair hair—her foster parents took her to another locality where she is now living and associating with White people."

Other cases of White women presenting husbands with Mulatto children are recorded. The husband of one of them "was absent from home for some time, and the woman bore a Mulatto child." Having given other similar cases one of them from Stafford County (on file in the State records) in which both the wife and the daughter of a White man bore children for the same Negro, the writer adds, "The above case presents the most ghastly evidence of the increasing frequency of the birth of mix-breed children to White women—formerly such cases were rare and even among the lowest grades of Whites."

Zeal of No Avail

Of another district the writer says: "Although no district in the state excels the Ninth in zeal for race integrity, the infrequency of the danger has resulted in a proportionate relaxation of watchfulness in guarding the color line. Hence Negroid, near-Whites from West Virginia and Kentucky, Negroid mixed

Indians from Tennessee, 'Red-bones' and self-styled 'Cherokees' from North Carolina have easily succeeded in 'passing.' A similar situation exists along particularly the whole southern border of the state—we have seen already how rapidly mix-breed descendants of one individual can multiply and how easily and widely they may be distributed."

After having other cases of Indians discovered to be of mixed White and Negro ancestry the writer cites the case of a Negro who after the Civil War, "came to Y county and bought the home of a prominent family. Three granddaughters of this man have married White men. These White men are of prominent families and well-connected. One of them has no children. These two men and their prominent kinspeople are exerting great pressure—successfully—to force their children into the most refined and cultured associations. They even had the assurance to send a lawyer to Richmond in 1924 to use his influence to prevent the passage of the racial integrity law.

"This case offers additional evidence that social position and wealth give no assured protection against the infusion of Negroid blood. What has happened to these families in Y County may happen to any family in Virginia."

In his summary and conclusion Powell says in part:

"The purpose of the foregoing article has been to show that the forces leading to amalgamation are not confined to isolated communities in the State but are common to all ten congressional districts and are general in their distribution. We have seen that the spread of the evil has not been merely geographical, but social, until it has, in a few instances, shown itself in every register of the social gamut. Most astonishing has been the evidence discovered of the disintegration of the psychological basis of the color line, namely, racial self respect and decency, as seen in cases of White men marrying Colored women and a White woman marrying or illicitly interbreeding with Colored men."

"This is the most appalling and threatening feature of the situation, and immediate steps for the control must be taken. The color line in America has been more permanent than in any other instance in history. The reason for this has been the strong tendency to place all mixed breeds on the Colored side of the barrier. Until recently the overwhelming majority of mixbreeds have been to Colored women; and as the law provided that illegitimate children take the color of the mother, these mixbreeds even when possessing sufficient White blood for White classification, were regarded as Colored. The situation changes, however, when the illegitimate mixbreeds are born of White mothers. The evidence of the increase of this crime among White women cannot be taken too seriously. Equally revolting is the complaisance shown in some of the cases by the White husbands of such women."

"Why drag forth from its concealment all this filth and rottenness to the offense of sensitive eyes and dainty nostrils? God is good and verily all men are brothers. Let us ignore what is unpleasant, or at least recognize it only to the extent of applying a coat of whitewash. There are many who think and speak in this manner."

"Incomparable folly! When has whitewash ever proved efficacious—"

Now the above expose' by Powell is a graphic picture of what has been going on in Virginia and throughout the South for the last three hundred years. And going on, too, in spite of all that an equally long line of Powells, Coxes, Copelands, Bleases, Tillmans, Vardamans, Dixons, have been able to do.

This thing, to anyone possessing an intellect above the prehistoric grade of a rhinoceros would then appear as fixed in nature, and nature, as the poet says, though driven out with a pitchfork, will always return. Men and women, who meet every day, even if they do meet only as servant and master, are going to have their likes and dislikes, their loves and hates, and their intimate associations. Will passing a law—a thousand laws hinder this?

This type, though it has pared its heels and pared its toes has been about as effective in preventing race-mixing as the cur that runs yelping after an express train or a prohibition agent who sets out to take the gin out of Virginia. Whether race mixing is good or bad, is entirely out of the question. One thing is sure that men of this type have succeeded in doing but one thing: in fostering a tremendous amount of immorality. They are promoters of bad citizenship. Inheritors of the slave-holding spirit, they are doing all they can to tighten the chains of economic and sexual slavery on their fellow citizens, for no other reason than a difference of complexion.

Their so-called African colonization plan they well know can serve only as a decoy for ignorant and gullible Negroes. Virginia took perhaps the lead in making it difficult for the Northern labor agent to recruit labor during the great Negro migration. Now it is going to have a change of mind to the extent of furnishing millions of dollars to send them "back" to Africa!

The great objective of the men above mentioned has been to keep the White woman out of the mixing, and they have failed, signally according to historical records. At one time there was a law that the White woman who married a Negro, became a slave for life with her husband, and that so worked as but to encourage such marriages. (See documentary evidence in "Beginnings of Miscegenation", Journal of Negro History.)

Hundreds of similar laws have been passed.

The law habit is but another dope habit. "Pass the bill," wailed Copeland to the Senate, "or we're lost!" "Just one shot more," pleads the dope fiend, "and I'll be a man again."

Some day the South is going to see that the only right way, the only moral way is to encourage marriage among all its citizens. The present prospects are, however, that it will realize this too late, like the man in the story, who had racked his mind to recall where he had hidden a large sum of money, and remembered it only after he had fallen overboard and was going down for the last time. Better, it is said, that the White race should perish first.

THE AMAZING PROGRESS OF THE BANKERS' FIRE INSURANCE CO.

Pittsburgh Courier
April 10, 1926
J. A. Rogers

DURHAM, N. C. Apr. 8.—How a Colored fire insurance company starting with little experience and at a most trying period, trebled its capital and is ranked today with many of the leading White firms of America in honesty and efficiency, all in five years, is the amazing achievement of the Bankers' Fire Insurance Company of Durham, North Carolina, whose offices I had the recent pleasure of visiting.

On consulting Best's Insurance Guide for 1925—world recognized authority—I found this Colored firm, which is perhaps the only one of its kind, had been given the highest possible rating for paying its fire losses. In management, it received a rating equal with scores of leading White firms, one of which has been in operation more than a century. Among these are: The Central Fire of Baltimore, 1865; Detroit Fire and Marine, 1866; Stuyvesant Fire of New York, 1850; Insurance Company of the State of Pennsylvania, 1794; and the Eagle Star of London, England, with assets of five million. Several big firms were rated lower than this Colored one, one of them being one of New York's greatest with assets of sixty million. Surely this is an accomplishment of which Negroes everywhere may well be proud.

The company was organized at a time when there were unfortunate happenings to corporations owned and controlled by Negroes, yet it has made such splendid headway that it has paid a dividend of four dollars on each share for the last three consecutive years. And as proof that when the Negro succeeds in business White firms are ready to recognize it is an offer from one of the large general agencies in Baltimore, one from a large general agency in Tennessee, one from Arkansas, one from New York, and one from New Jersey, to act as representatives for Bankers' Fire in those states.

The firm owns the modern three story building in which it is located, has assets of nearly four hundred thousand dollars, and policies of over eleven million dollars, part of which is reinsured in reputable White companies.

At the annual meeting held in the Home Office on March 11, the annual report showed that the company had entered one additional state—Arkansas—in 1925. The report also showed that in writing automobile insurance covering fire and theft only, the company had not had a single loss on this class of business. Tornado insurance has also been authorized by the Board of Directors.

The officers are: W. G. Pearson, president; C. C. Spaulding, vice president, and J. M. Avery, treasurer. The last two are president and treasurer respectively of the North Carolina Mutual Life Insurance Company. The Secretary-Manager is W. Gomez, who possesses a personal letter of commendation from the Best's Guide Company for the excellent manner in which the business has been conducted. The system was installed by L. W. Wilhoite, who has been the acting auditor since the organization of the company. R. N. Harris is managing underwriter and H. W. Hill, special representative. The clerical work is done by a staff of efficient young Colored women.

It is encouraging to note that this is a progressive organization along all lines. At the recent meeting the stockholders, one of the most pleasant surprises came to a worthy young man—L. W. Wilhoite—who could hardly believe it when he was notified that he had been elected to the Board of Directors of the company. The Manager, W. Gomez, in presenting him for election to the stockholders said , among other things: "We must recognize ability and give the merited places to these worthy young men who are giving their lives to foster our corporations."

J. A. ROGERS TELLS US OF SOUTHERN HUMANITY

Pittsburgh Courier
July 10, 1926
J. A. Rogers

North Carolina has the reputation of being the most civilized of the Southern States. In many quarters it is fondly believed that the race question has been solved and that all the Colored people are happy; but an incident happened here last week that for sheer heartlessness would disgrace even Georgia or Mississippi: Shelley Lee, 38, a barber of Burlington, N. C., with a shop catering only to White people, closed up his place after midnight Saturday, and was standing outside, when he was attacked by a bandit, who shot him through the abdomen, robbed him and fled.

Instead of admitting him to the local hospital, the authorities at Burlington, rushed him to Durham, forty miles away in an ambulance. He arrived there in great agony at 2:00 a.m. Dr. J. W. Cordice at once sewed up the wounds in his abdomen and intestines but Shelley died before morning.

Dr. Cordice says that but for the loss of blood, and the shaking caused by the long, hurried ride, Shelley might have been saved.

Burlington has the reputation of being a regular cracker town. In passing through the town one sees a sign bidding him a hearty Rotarian Welcome.

A similar incident happened to Miss Marjorie Shepard, daughter of Dr. James E. Shepard, President of the North Carolina College for Negroes of this town recently. She was motoring with a party of friends through Lexington, N.C., when the car went into a ditch. She was badly hurt and her arm broken in two places but she had to come on here for first aid. The only Colored doctor in the town was away, and the White doctors refused to give her first aid.

ROGERS VISITS MARCUS GARVEY IN ATLANTA PRISON

Talks To Prisoner No. 19,359 One Hour; Garvey Admits He Will Be Deported On Release

---

U.N.I.A. Head Dressed in Blue Uniform; Is Thinner, But Healthy; Has Plenty Of Time To Read.

The Pittsburgh Courier
November 20, 1926
J. A. Rogers
Author "From Superman to Man"
[The Pittsburgh Courier's Editor's Note: Mr. Rogers is on a tour of the South, lecturing and selling his books.]

ATLANTA, Ga., November 18.—In coming to this city I had among other objectives two rather itching ones: to see the home of His Majesty, the Imperial Wizard of the Ku Klux Klan, the White king of America; and to see the Black king, or more correctly, the provisional President of Africa, Marcus Garvey. Sunday last, taking the Jim Crow car I rode out six miles on Peachtree Road and saw the former, an imitation White House, nesting in an oaken grove; and a few days later, piloted by two of the fine friends I have met here, Drs. C. Waymond Reeves and J. B. Brown, I motored over to the magnificent university-like building with the beautiful sweep of lawn, that is the federal penitentiary to see the latter.

Appearing at the barred gate under the great Doric columns we were politely ushered by the guard to a desk where we gave our names and after a short wait, and with much less formality than we had expected, were conducted through a heavy, iron-barred door into a room where after another short wait we saw the stocky figure of the originator of the first world movement among Negroes enter, clad in what appears to be the garb of any ordinary laborer hereabouts—trousers of bluish material, red sweater, and loose cap of thin dark material, nothing to indicate a prisoner in popular belief—but an unbelievable contrast to the figure in the glittering uniform, golden epaulets, plumed hat, sword and spurs on the prancing steed which as leader of the "400,000,000 Negroes of the World" led his followers through the streets of Harlem in 1921.

Responding to our cordial greetings with equal warmth, he took a seat facing us with the guard nearby, and opened the conversation with a remark about my recent trip to Europe. My being refused permission to visit Africa seemed a sore point with him. "Why," said he, "if there is any place a Negro ought to be allowed to go it is Africa." He went on to speak of the world wide attempt being made to Jim Crow Negroes, and touched on the laws recently passed barring Colored people from Brazil, Mexico and Panama, declaring that Negroes, particularly those of the Western world were getting just what they deserved for their lethargy. "Soon they won't be able to travel at all, then perhaps they will wake up," he said.

I went on to tell him how hundreds of persons in England and France, some of them prominent, had asked me about him: of how many Negroes in this country, some of them wealthy, who sympathized with him; and of the discussion of himself and of his movement that I knew were taking place in many of our colleges, at which he seemed quite pleased. There is much about Garveyism with which I, for one radically disagree, as for instance his approval of the narrow racialism of such insidious enemies of America and the Negro, as Cox, Powell, and the Ku Klux Emperor, yet the simple truth remains that there is considerable sympathy for him, sometimes, as I have found, in quite unexpected places. Although his followers have dwindled in actual members he is the most widely discussed Negro in the world today. Two recent missionaries from Africa, one of them a man for whom I hold the highest respect, told me of the hold that Garveyism was taking in Africa that was a revelation to me.

And as I listened to Convict No. 19,395 speak in his resolute, well informed way of the doings in the world of Negroes—of affairs in Abyssinia, South Africa, Liberia, the West Indies, Brazil, as well as of India, Egypt, and the League of Nations, I realized that Garveyism is still very much alive. Of his original program he has evidently yielded not one step. "When I get out of here," he said with all that old fire that had held his great audiences spellbound in Madison Square Garden, "I mean to do a thousand times more." This was in direct answer to a question about his steamship program. These activities, however, will take place on British territory, unless Uncle Sam relents, as according to Garvey, himself, his deportation is settled.

The self-appointed ruler of Africa is considerably thinner. Gone is most of his paunch and beefy shoulders, but he looks several years younger in the pink of health. Time, he says, does not hang heavily, as he has abundant time for reading after duties, which, he said, he was not permitted to name. "Before I came in here," he said, quite cheerfully, "I had no time whatever for reading, but now I can keep well-posted on everything," and he evidently does. This, of course, is as near as I can recall his words as I was stopped by the guard when I took out the paper and began to write.

Number 19,359—the Harlem policy fans might try that—feels that he has not been fairly treated by that part of the Negro people who opposed his movement. Such he declared, had never looked into his program, but had based their objections on rumor, or on what his enemies had said. As to the latter, he charged, that they had first called him a "nobody," then later a "West Indian," and when he still continued to gain following, "a crook." As to the two volumes of "His Philosophy and Opinions" he said that the Negro press had been silent about it while his wife had a scrapbook filled with clippings from the White press here and in Europe.

The N. A. A. C. P.

When I asked him what he thought of the N. A. A. C. P. he said that he thought it was an excellent and highly necessary movement, but that the leadership was wrong, declaring that the present leaders were only interested in succeeding themselves in office, and pushing only those cases that would bring them plenty of notoriety. "The N. A. A. C. P." he said, "encourages Negroes to move into White neighborhoods, and to do such things as got the Sweets into trouble, then turns around and cashes in on them." For this remark I felt that the advocates of residential segregation in Washington, D.C., and elsewhere, would give him plenty of publicity.

As to the $5,000 given to Dr. Du Bois for the study of Negro education, is it in the South or South Carolina?—and which appeared in the September Crisis, he wanted to know why that sum should have been necessary since Du Bois had lived in the South and was familiar with conditions there. .He was plainly elated at the articles appearing in the Pittsburgh Courier. "Vann," he said, "has dragged to light facts which I had long felt to be true."

Of Liberia, he said President King had deceived him, gladly accepting him at first, but ousting him for bigger game. As to the Firestone Company he said, that it would have been better had Liberia only leased the land, but as things now were it should try to get the tire company under governmental control.

Regarding the rumor of his not being permitted to return to Jamaica, West Indies, he said, that there had been similar talk in 1921, but he had visited all the places it was said he could not go and had returned to America without any trouble. It was at this point he complained of the "baseless rumors perpetually floated about him," one of which was that President Coolidge had offered him a pardon if he would leave the country.

As to his first wife, he said, she was motivated by "pure notoriety" and that he had been legally divorced from her prior to his second marriage. When I suggested that he would have fared better had he got a lawyer, he insisted that here for once the maxim that the man who is his own lawyer has a fool for a client was wrong, as if he had not done so he would have got "sixty years" as there was much on the inside that an onlooker would never have understood.

At the end of an hour the guard warned us that our time was up and No. 19,359 returned to what will be his home for another two years at least, while the three of us passed again through the iron gates to see again the magnificent lawn, and the wooded expanse in all the glory and gold of an Indian summer. I for one, absorbed in the thought that the once humble West Indian peasant who had just disappeared behind the clanging gates had started something that liked or hated, is destined to affect the future of humanity in no mean way.

HARLEM'S SHERLOCK HOLMES—HERBERT S. BOULIN

Nemesis of Unfaithful Husbands Has Solved Murder Mysteries, Jewelry Thefts, Insurance Frauds, Political Plots and Fake Suits

Pittsburgh Courier
February 5, 1927
J. A. Rogers

Known mostly to newspaper readers as an avenger of Cupid and the nemesis of unfaithful husbands and wives, Herbert S. Boulin, Harlem's own Sherlock Holmes, has had, nevertheless, a career as unique and fascinating as Conan Doyle's famous character. Like Sherlock Holmes, he has solved murder mysteries, jewelry thefts, insurance frauds, political plots, fake suits against railroads, worked on news beats for some of the city's leading papers, and, strangest of all to the ears of those accustomed to read of his bursting into the bedroom of some unfaithful man or woman at midnight with his raiding party, will come the story that on several occasions he has served as the vindicator of oppressed Negro womanhood.

For instance, the following incident, involving the loss of a diamond necklace valued at $25,000: This necklace, which was the birthday gift of a rich manufacturer whom we will call Mr. Cohen, to his wife, suddenly disappeared one day. The insurance company was called upon to make good, and it hired Boulin.

Defender of Women

On taking the case he discovered that the Cohens had two homes, one at Long Beach, the other on Riverside Drive. In the family were one child, one White nursemaid and a Colored houseworker we will call Jenny, who had been with the Cohens three years. When the family went to Long Beach for the summer, Jenny stayed to care for the Riverside Drive home.

One day the Cohens gave a party at Long Beach and Jenny was called in to cook and otherwise help, with the result that when the affair was over it was too late for her to return to the city, and she spent the night there. Next morning, while Jenny was in the kitchen, Mrs. Cohen rushed in, greatly agitated, and demanded of her what she had done with the necklace, as she felt sure she had given it to her to put away the night before. Strenuous denials from Jenny, and the search began. The Long Beach police were called in; the insurance company notified, with insinuations from Mrs. Cohen that Jenny was the thief. When Boulin came on the job, Mrs. Cohen repeated her suspicions to him. Jenny, she said, had diamonds of her own, played the numbers and the horses, kept another room outside, and had property in Baltimore. In short, in the eyes of the Cohen family, the insurance company and the police, there was little doubt that Jenny was the thief. And had there been the least doubt, there was Jenny's color.

A sleuth from Boulin's agency soon got in touch with Jenny, took her to theatres, dances, dinners and for a month and a half checked her up and down, discovering some queer things.

The detective found that Jenny had not only one outside room, but two, one in Ninety-ninth street and the other on Sixty-third street. Moreover, she did play the numbers and the horses, had jewelry, and property in Baltimore, and kept late hours, going to some affair almost every night, but being always on the job to get the Cohen's breakfast at seven. She lived such a fast life that the detective was pretty well worn out keeping up with her.

But this was what he found: At one of the rooms she kept her jewelry and a trunk, paying nominal rent; at the other she entertained her friends. In time the detective had so won her confidence that she was showing him her jewelry, of which the sleuth made careful mental note. He had further been instructed to look out for some valuable rings, missing from the Cohen's two years before, for which another insurance company had had to make good.

Months passed and the detectives, finding no pawn-tickets or any other proof of Jenny's guilt, decided she was innocent. The White nursemaid also had been carefully checked, and nothing found against her. Shortly after the loss, Mrs. Cohen had given her leave and she had returned to her home in Canada, whither Boulin detectives had followed her.

With the two maids eliminated, suspicion could be directed in only one place, and this the insurance company was strongly inclined not to accept, as the Cohens were wealthy and of fine reputation. Jenny remained the suspect.

Up to this point Jenny hadn't any suspicion that she had been actually accused of the theft, and now Boulin decided to play other cards. One night, while she and her detective escort were coming out of a theatre, Boulin, accompanied by another detective, accused her openly of the theft, and there followed a fake fight in which the detective escort was beaten. Then was played the trump. Boulin then told her where he had got his information, adding for good luck that he had heard even worse things about her, which was that she was keeping a sporting house in Philadelphia. Enraged, Jenny wanted to know who was the informant, and was finally told it was Mrs. Cohen.

But, said Boulin later to her: "I suspect that Mrs. Cohen is the thief." Jenny, eager for revenge, became a detective against her mistress on the spot, and began to tell things that immediately threw another light on the matter.

Among them was that Mrs. Cohen was always attending bridge parties, losing heavily at times; also, that another woman had been visiting her recently, showing diamond bracelets. Jenny got the names of Mrs. Cohen's bridge friends and turned them in.

Jenny also divulged another secret; namely, that the rings that were missing two years before had been stolen by Mrs. Cohen's brother, who had taken them out West, had pawned them and sent her the tickets, after which the insurance company had paid the loss. Mrs. Cohen was also planning a trip to Europe as soon as the insurance company had made good for the necklace.

The woman with the bracelets had made two visits to the Cohen home, and Jenny was now directed to search for any possible bills for them, and although she could hardly read finally brought Boulin a bill for six bracelets that had been made at a cost of two thousand dollars. A photostat of the bill was made, after which Jenny returned the original to Mrs. Cohen's drawer.

Months passed. Mrs. Cohen's brother in California was traced, the pawn-tickets recovered, and one day Mr. Cohen was called to the office of the insurance company.

Husband Called In

"Are you still willing to do all in your power to recover your wife's necklace?" Mr. Cohen was asked.

Cohen insisted that he was as determined as ever to

punish the thief.

"Would you be surprised to learn," he was told, "that your wife had something to do with it?"

Cohen was indignant at the supposed insult, insisted that Jenny was the thief, and that he had kept her on only on the advice of the detectives.

"Did you give Mrs. Cohen a number of bracelets recently?" asked Boulin.

Another denial. There was presented the photostat of the bill for the bracelets, the pawn-tickets for the missing rings, tales also of his wife's losses at bridge. Collapse of Mr. Cohen, who was forced to choose between having his wife arrested for grand larceny and conspiracy or paying all the expenses of the investigation, returning the money paid on insurance for the rings, a promise never again to seek jewelry insurance, and to cancel all such policies then in force. He chose the latter, and Mrs. Cohen, getting wind of the affair from the jeweler, fled to Europe, avoiding her husband.

As to the missing necklace, Mrs. Cohen had given it to a woman fence to have it cut down into the bracelets, thereby forever changing its identity.

Suspicion Often Directed at Domestics to Cover Up Conspiracy to Collect Insurance Money—Poison Pen Letter Writer Nabbed, Typewriter and All

Falsely Accused

Still another case was that of a Colored woman who had been hired less than an hour before from an employment agency to do some cleaning. While working in the bathroom, this maid was suddenly confronted with a policeman, who accused her of stealing jewelry valued at $5,000, the property of the lady we will call Mrs. Isaacs, who had just hired her. The maid protested her innocence, but she was made to strip then and there in front of the policeman, Mrs. Isaacs' son and daughter, and Mrs. Isaacs, herself, while her clothes were searched.

The insurance company seemed faced with no alternative but paying the loss, but called in Boulin. Taking the four members of the Isaacs family apart, he questioned them separately, everyone giving a different story as to the movements of the maid and the time.

The jimmy mark on the bureau drawer with the jewelry was even pointed out by Mrs. Isaacs.

Another Inside Job

Another suspicious thing; neither Mr. nor Mrs. Isaacs could say where the jewelry had been bought; moreover, it was discovered that the jewelry in question had been insured less than a month, and that not even the binding amount had been paid. Cornered, Isaacs finally agreed to waive all claims.

At the present time a heavy suit is pending against Isaacs in the civil courts for his indignities to the maid. Boulin saw to it that her case was put in the hands of a competent Colored lawyer.

Poison Pen

Yet another case was that of a school teacher on a vacation visit to New York City, with whom a certain New Yorker fell in love. She, it appears, did not return his love, and to get even he sent anonymous letters to her principal accusing her of misconduct, as well as others to her friends, declaring that she had given him a social disease.

The young lady was soon a nervous wreck, but some of her friends took the matter up and placed it in the hands of Boulin who began by listing all her acquaintances in New York City. All the letters had been written on the same typewriter, sometimes there were three of them in a day.

Narrowing down the suspects to one, Boulin finally tracked the man to his home cornered him, and found the typewriter and unsent letters. Because of the delicate nature of the case no exposure was made. The man made a complete retraction, ending a harrowing experience for the girl.

The man, often seen on the streets of Harlem now, had spent four months in a psychopathic ward in Bellevue Hospital.

* * *

Next week will be told how the romance of a son of one of America's most prominent families with a poor girl led to a contest between two millionaires for a seat in the United States Senate and a bid for the Negro vote, together with how Boulin was called in.

COLOR LINE WITHIN RACE FUTILE

West Indian Writer Hits "Blue Vein" Worshippers Who Take Pride In Illegitimate Ancestry

Says American White Man's Policy of Forcing All Shades Into One Group Will Be Salvation of Race.

The Pittsburgh Courier
March 19, 1927
J. A. Rogers

{Pittsburgh Courier's Editor's Note: This is the last of Mr. Rogers' articles written exclusively for The Pittsburgh Courier before he sailed on February 22, for North Africa. The Courier expects to publish his first article from abroad at an early date. Mr. Rogers himself is of mixed blood.}

NEW YORK, March 17.—Speaking recently to a group of White students, I told them that there was something about the possession of color prejudice by White people that amused me immensely, since I had met Colored people who could beat them at their own game.

I told them about the West Indies, and the Island of Jamaica, in particular, where instead of two color casts as in the United States, there are three: White, Colored, and Black. This can be noted in all census reports of the islands. Thee, the Whites, a very small minority not a total of five percent of the two million or so people in the British West Indies, have deliberately taught the people of mixed blood—"Colored"—as they are called, that they are better than the Blacks giving them the preference in such governmental jobs that are given the natives. Some years ago, civil service examinations were abolished in Jamaica and appointments by the governor substituted. The reason for this was that there were too many Blacks getting in. The Blacks constitute at least 85 percent of the population of that island.

Whiteness in the West Indies, as in America, and South Africa, is a system of exploitation, and in order to keep on top, the Whites, few in number, very cleverly seized on the nearest shades of color to themselves, the Mulattoes, and erected them into a superior caste—a caste, not equal with themselves, of course, but a little lower than the angels. And because the Mulattoes are just as much human as the Whites, the Blacks, the Pinks, or any other shade of humanity, they seized on this squalid form of distinction, eagerly manifesting toward the Blacks the snobbishness one might find in a Southern Cracker who objects to the presence of a Negro in a Pullman or a public dining room. There is, of course, the fact that the Black West Indian can not be legally barred in his home—a condition that perhaps makes it all the more exasperating for many of the near-Whites.

I could give innumerable instances of this color prejudice on the part of Mulattoes toward Black, but will confine myself to a single instance. I can well recall as a boy of seven, in Jamaica, a certain Mulatto, who was so injudicious as to follow his heart and marry a Black woman was pointed out to me as a horrible example of a social misfortune. This man's family was simply not received by its Colored relatives, just as in America, if the man were White, his family would not be received by his White relatives. Of course this is not to say such is always the case. Some few White foreigners have married Black women in the West Indies and these have been received in their husband's circles. The "pure" White in the West Indies, broadly speaking, belongs to the local aristocracy.

And so, after citing this and other instances, I said to

the group of White students: "Now if looking down upon other people because of color is a smart thing to do, how can the White American be so superior when the West Indian Negro whom he would look down upon can equal, even eclipse him in doing the same thing?"

In America, more than once a Mulatto male has told me that he would never think of marrying a Black woman. Here, however, because the Whites are numerous, and have no need of Mulattoes to bolster up their system of exploitation, the dictum is that if one has "one drop" of so-called Negro blood he is a Negro. Hence all the different complexions of Negroes are thrown together, willy-nilly. In the West Indies the man with "a drop" and even more would be inclined to repudiate indignantly his Negro ancestry, while in America he will often gladly acknowledge it. This, however, is not because he is a superior, moral creature, but because his interest lies forcibly with the Negro group. If he were discovered among the Whites he would be cast out with no other refuge but the Negro caste.

In the West Indies the light-Colored girl will rarely think of marrying a Black man. In America the tendency is the other way about. It is a common sight to see Colored women as white as many White people, married to a Black man. Perhaps the reason for this is that since whiteness is the standard of beauty and economic preference in America, for both Negroes and Caucasians, the Black man picks out the light woman so that in the event of children, the latter will start life with less handicaps than himself.

And so race prejudice helps to break down the very caste system so hard to maintain, for it thus brings about a perpetual lightening of color, which in its final analysis serves to increase the number of near-Whites who "cross over." There is this one thing to be thankful for about ignorance: it never fails to defeat its own ends.

After all the American method of dark men marrying light women is better, because it helps to destroy that inter-color caste which is the bane of Negro progress in the West Indies. The Negroes there, as was said, outnumber the Whites nineteen to one, yet the Whites remain on top largely by using the Mulattoes as a monkey to pull their chestnuts out of the fire.

In some parts of America, notably Richmond, Washington and Charleston, there are so-called blue-veined societies, but these are not only ridiculous, but pathetic. Pride of family as it exists among the Whites, and other peoples, has as its basis so-called legitimacy—it is founded on marriage. Trace, however, the ancestry of almost every one of these "blue veins" and it goes back to illegitimacy, to the union of a Black woman and a White man, so that in every instance when a lighter-Colored person looks down upon a darker-Colored person, and, refuses to acknowledge him as an equal, that light-Colored person is really despising himself, or to be exact, despising a part of himself. And if a house divided against itself cannot stand, how can an individual divided against himself ever hope to?

Speaking of pride of ancestry, whether it be descent from White people, from kings, dukes or other warts on the body politic, it is usually a sign of the inferiority complex. As some wit once said: "The man who boasts of his ancestry is like a potato plant; the best part of him is underground."

The great curse of this color situation, not only in West Indies, but in America, is that the average Negro thinks white. The White man so acts as to make the Negro feel that it is whiteness of skin in itself, that has put him temporarily on top, and many Negroes, dead from the jaw-bone up, swallow that falsehood whole. As I pointed in my book—"From 'Super-Man' to Man," if whiteness of skin alone counted for anything, then a side of pork hanging in a butcher shop was equal to a White man, for both are of the same color. As I said then, there are few Caucasian beauties who can equal the rosy, dainty freshness of a newly shaved sucking-pig. As to hair, there never yet was a monkey without straight hair, and thin lips. Many gorillas have hair as red and as silky as an Irish beauty. Many apes have faces as white as any White person, hence the little African boy mentioned in Darwin's "Decent of Man," certainly knew what he was talking about when he exclaimed on seeing a White man: "Look at the White man! Does he not look like a white ape?"

After all, no matter what differences may exist among Negroes, political, religious, commercial, individual, there is one point on which nearly every one can agree, namely, the desire for justice and opportunity. Hence, it seems to me, that the intelligent thing to do is to get together on this point, even if it be necessary to hold on to the other differences. But of these differences, to finish where we began, the most monkeyfied, with apologies to the monkey, is that of taking pride in sharing the ancestry of the oppressor—a trait, it seems, that is peculiar only to Negroes.

"AFRICA DIFFERENT FROM BOOK DESCRIPTION" SAYS J. A. ROGERS

American Writers Lands In Morocco After 9 Days Out; Comments On Trip Across

Says Captain of Ship Read Copy of Courier With Interest; Casablanca Is "Quite White."

The Pittsburgh Courier
April 2, 1927
J. A. Rogers

{Pittsburgh Courier's Editor's Note: This is the beginning of Mr. Rogers' first article from North Africa, where he is at present making an observation tour. Mr. Rogers sailed Feb. 22 from New York and landed in Casablanca, March 3. Those wishing to write him may address him at 11 Rue Scribe, c/o American Express Co., Paris France, and his mail will be forwarded from there. He will be pleased to hear from any one interested in his trip, and will be pleased to make any special observations that may be requested of him, providing it is convenient for him to do so. He will be abroad about a year.}

CASABLANCA, Morocco, French North Africa, March 5.—Crossing the North Atlantic at almost its widest part, straight across New York City to Africa, curving around the Azores to reach Casablanca on the Moroccan coast, is a long and tiresome journey. Tradition says that this vast waste of water, that now takes nine days in crossing was all land once—the continent of Atlantis. One wishes heartily, after the first three days out, that terra firma had remained, for if one has evolved very far from the fishes, he will prefer the train any day. Hurry up airplanes!

Yet, let the mind fly backward a bit, and one will find that he really has nothing to kick about. Seventy years ago one would have been lucky to make the trip in twenty-nine days;

and a hundred and fifty years back—well, one had to wait on the wind!

I thought also of the trip further to the South, that our Negro ancestors were forced to make, battened under hatches, crowded and crazed with intolerable heat and thirst, and then of myself in a fairly comfortable cabin, third class though it was. I thought also of the manner in which the ancestors of many of our proud American Nordics crossed, much of this same route—how they also came over in slave-ships, sometimes the majority of them dying just like the Africans, from overcrowding. That is a shameful chapter in his ancestry that the White American is anxious to suppress, but let one read, for instance, Faust's "German Element in the United States," or Gustavus Myers' "History of the U.S. Supreme Court," for documentary evidence. With the demand for labor in the American colonies, English boys and girls were kidnapped in such large number and sold into slavery in America and the West Indies that Parliament finally had to fix a penalty of death "without benefit of clergy" for the kidnappers.

Africa, or at least the part of it I have seen in the past few days, is so astonishingly different from what I had imagined from my reading, that, indeed, I feel as if I had been taken bodily and put into another world. Morocco, whose history antedates the Romans, is called "The Classic Land of the Arabian Nights." To get some idea of the permanence of its ways and customs, read again your "Arabian Nights' Entertainments," for, evidently, things have changed little, if any, in a thousand years. I shall try my best to communicate to my readers some of the things I have seen, some of the surprises I have felt, but I shall be fortunate, indeed, if I succeed in conveying a tenth of it.

Much of what I am going to say might not prove so palatable to our good folk, radical, conservative, and otherwise—I think I have a little kick coming myself because several of my pet notions have been shattered-nevertheless, I am going to tell of things just as I have seen them, neither more nor less.

The Trip Across

But to proceed in regular order I must tell something of the trip across, and of the folk I met. The last time I took an American ship I met mostly Nordics; this time I took an Italian ship, with every person in third class brunette with black hair, and myself, again the only one to whom the English language was native (all the rest Italian). The last time, when I went to Europe, with those Americanized Nordics it was "Nigger, Nigger;" nothing of the sort this trip. It was "Colored lady" and "Colored gentleman" when they spoke of the Colored folk with whom they had worked, or who had traded with them.

All belong to the laboring or the petty trading classes and are neither cleaner nor dirtier than the Nordics, indeed, they seem a little less odorous, but the comparison is hardly fair since I had the Nordics in the summer. The average intelligence seems about the same, and the amiability and cheerfulness, important factors in good citizenship, much higher than the Nordics—hereafter I shall have to be careful about calling Colored folk "noisy." All in all, the favoring of the North European in the immigration quota seems to me more than ever a case of the White folk drawing "the color line" within their own ranks.

As to the opinion of many of my fellow passengers regarding America, that will prove interesting. America, they think, is a fine place for making money, but little else. No freedom, no culture, no knowledge of how to enjoy life, they declare. Many have saved enough to serve for the rest of their lives, and are returning to the land, where "things are things." Some with large families are returning because they say it is simply impossible to make ends meet with eight or nine children in America—wouldn't I just like to place the opponents of birth control in the exact place of some of these poor mothers and fathers I saw on the ship? One mother, travelling alone, has three children, all unable to help themselves, and is expecting another. Her husband is sending her home. Others are going home to see their wives and children, while the majority, so far as I can gather, are returning to visit. Most of them are naturalized.

As to prohibition, it may be imagined one gets a ready hearing when he speaks about it. The first meal served on the ship was "dry," but at all the others, wine flowed far freer than water. "Watta swella da bell. Make you take too much medicine," confided one man, who drinks a quart bottle full of wine with each of the two meals. Still, no one is drunk. The Latin, reared on wine, holds his liquor like a gentleman; your Anglo-Saxon needs prohibition to make and keep him respectable.

The ship and all about it are as clean as human effort can make it, but the food, while wholesome, was far from being to my taste. One thing I have learnt at last: The proper way to eat spaghetti, but if I can help it I am going to see that that knowledge doesn't do me any good for a long time to come.

I had the great pleasure of meeting one of the officers of the ship, Dr. Giacomo Vesceglia, a young man, graduate of two leading Italian universities. I went up to his office on business, and when he learnt that I was a writer it was most interesting to see the remarkable change in his face. He invited me in, offered me a seat, and we chatted for hours. Why was I travelling third class, he wanted to know? Since then he has been most kind. I have cited this instance merely to illustrate what I have already pointed out, namely, the high respect accorded the professional man in Europe, regardless of color. I showed him a copy of

The Courier, which he read with great interest. He particularly noted its size. The Courier, it must be explained, is almost twice the size of the European newspaper, with the exception of two or three London papers which are, perhaps, a little smaller than The Courier.

Casablanca

To return to Morocco. My first impression of Casablanca from the ship was that of entering some modern American sea-port, except that Casablanca is quite White, just like its name, which is Spanish for "white house." Whitewashing is a fetish with the Moors. Overhead was the bluest skies I have ever seen, which came down to meet a sea so blue itself that it was almost difficult to tell the horizon, while over the mountains, back toward the great desert, were the strangest masses of fleecy white clouds, suggesting flocks of enormous sheep. Entering the town one is reminded, but for its newness, of Paris. Smart French shops with the latest styles, the terraces of the cafes just as on the grand boulevards crowded with patrons sipping wine or coffee, the banks, and the hordes of taxis, with the honking peculiar to the French cab.

(Continued next week. In the second part of this article, to be published next week, Mr. Rogers gives a vivid, picturesque description of the people and street scenes in Casablanca. It will prove most interesting. Don't miss it. Mr. Rogers' observations may appear in other newspapers, but by special arrangement with him, a more extended and detailed account of his travels will appear only in The Pittsburgh Courier. So be sure to read what Mr. Rogers has to say in this newspaper.)

"I'M 3,000 MILES AWAY FROM THE COLOR LINE" — Writes J. A. Rogers

Religion Only Barrier American Observer Finds On His North African Tour

Says Men There Have As Many Wives As They Can Feed—From Jet-Black to Blonde.

The Pittsburgh Courier
April 9, 1927
J. A. Rogers

(Continued from Last Week)

Continuing his article on Casablanca, Morocco, French North Africa, Mr. Rogers writes:

But wait, all this is but a prelude to the strangest mélange of humanity I have ever seen. Step into the native quarter abutting the main street, and you step back a thousand years, further back yet, back into Bible times. The 20th Century A.D. rubbing elbows with the Second Century B.C. Winding its way in the narrow, tortuous streets among lurching camels, forlorn donkeys, and water carriers with skins filled with water, resembling bloated goats, minus the heads, are the latest style motor cars. Overhead a huge air-plane is humming.

Let me try to express as briefly as possible my first impression of this bewildering scene. Imagine a Ku Klux Konvention—Ku Kluxers of every possible human color, from that of coal to the blondest Nordic, and wearing instead of American shoes, sandals or bare feet. Open the hood so as to disclose some of the face, substitute a red fez here and there, add a policeman or soldier in uniform and you'll have the human ensemble.

And as to the ladies, they would need only the shoes, for all that one can see of them is their darkened eyes, red-stained finger tips and bare heels, Colored with black and red. Walking from the rear on Seventh Avenue in Harlem these days it is impossible to tell the grandmothers from the flappers; well, here you can't tell them at all. Of course, not all the women are thus swathed, but these, I was informed, are not the "good" women, which includes all Christians and Jews.

As to "the color line" one is three thousand miles or more away from it, straight as the crow flies, westward. Europe, Asia, and Africa meet here in one indiscriminating mélange, but for the barrier of religion. Again and again I would see a face that reminded me strongly of our Colored folk, but communication was out of the question, unless one spoke Arabic.

The Arab, as I said, has a fetish for whiteness, not of skin, but for covering of the body and the outside of the home. This was intended, no doubt, for hygienic reasons. The richer Arab keeps his garb and the outside of his home and courtyard very white. But for the poor, which swarm like flies, the habit but accentuates the dirt.

Go into an American rag shop, take out the dirtiest articles there, drag them through the streets for any length of time—a week, if you like, fit them to form a shroud for the body, and you'll have some idea of the state of the clothing worn in the poorer quarters. I must insist that I am not exaggerating. I have seen very, very dirty Negroes in the South; I have seen the squalor of the Shoshone Indians in Nevada, but never before have I seen misery and filth in such a mass. I was informed that some have never bathed from birth, and I could well believe it. Water, as I said, is sold on the streets. Head, leg, hand and eye sores are common. Scratch, scratch, scratch! When I expressed my surprise to a friend, who has been around the world, he shrugged his shoulders: "It's nothing," he said, "you ought to see Shanghai." Conditions described here apply to poor White and Black alike. I went to the homes of some of the very poorest, lean-to's of tins, and there was the same attempt at whitewashing. Hygienic conditions as may be imagined are very bad. With water sold on the streets there can be no sewage—a condition worse in the desert towns, where water is even scarcer than good liquor in America.

Food is handled in the same unsanitary way. Imagine going to your grocer, calling for butter, and he dips a very dirty hand into the keg and hands you out a gob of it. I, for one, would have to be dying from thirst, before I would touch a drop of water from the inside of one of those swollen goats. And in the summer I hear that all the flies from Pharaoh's plague are resurrected here.

And as to being religious, the Colored brother here can outdo the one in America, only their Gods have nothing in common. Of this I shall speak later.

Of course I have been speaking of the poorer natives, who seem to be in the great majority. The rich, I understand, live in luxury with harems. In this city, almost in the heart of the most squalid district is one of the palaces of the former Sultan, who was deposed by the French, after its capture and bombardment by them in 1907.

Yet, these people, fallen as they now are, were once the leading power in Europe, giving it one of the finest civilizations it ever had.

* * *

Rabat, Morocco

This city (Rabat, Morocco) north of Casablanca, is the official capital of French Morocco. It is here the Sultan resides, but to use an Americanism, he is only a "Yes Man"—the real ruler is Marshal Lyautey, the French governor. I was fortunate enough to arrive here on Friday, and saw the Sultan, accompanied by his bodyguard, going to midday worship. He is a dark complexioned man, and would easily be called a "Negro" in America. Rabat is older, more historic, and far less European than Casablanca, which is the commercial capital. One feels as if he had suddenly rubbed Aladdin's wonderful lamp, and been transported back 25 centuries. Rabat is, or was a walled town, with richly carved entrance, the most picturesque of which is the Medersa Gate. These entrances, worn by the feet of man and animals remind one of wave-beaten rocks. There is also the famous Hassan Tower, the Garden of Oudaya, and the ruined columns of what was once a great mosque (pronounced mos-kay), or church. To the east, in the far distance is Fez, the intellectual capital of the Moors, the centre of their arts, letters and music.

Fez will be of special interest to Negroes because it is the birthplace of Leo Africanus, a Negro who dazzled Europe with his learning and whose book, "History and Description of Africa," was the standard work on that continent for more than three hundred years. Leo, whose Moorish name I have forgotten, was captured by the slave traders, whose ship, in turn, was captured by the Genoese about 1510. Leo was taken to Italy, where he so delighted Pope Leo X that the latter became his god-father and patron. The only copy I have ever seen of this book was owned by Arthur A. Schomburg, and perhaps may be seen in his famous collection in New York City.

The Moors, though fallen pretty low now, like the Egyptians, Ethiopians, Greeks, and others, —perhaps Abdel-Krim, made the last famous stand—were once the principal power in Europe. I think it was Draper who said that the stables of the Arabian chargers of the Moorish kings of Spain were finer than the palaces of the then ruling kings of England. Of this I shall say more when I write of Gibraltar and Southern Spain.

It is difficult to speak with accuracy of the customs of a country whose language one does not speak, nevertheless, I have taken pains to get my information from the most reliable sources, native and French. I have been told polygamy prevails, and harems abound. Each Arab keeps as many wives as he can feed, though his Bible, the Koran, permits only four. The last Sultan had three hundred, it will be recalled. These wives, as a French lady, who says she has been in a harem, tells me, are of all shades of color, from jet-black to blonde. There is absolutely no color line—a fact evident on the streets. And if a Black slave woman becomes the mother of a child, or a White one for that matter, the child shares equally with those of the legal wives, and has the same political and social privileges, just as in Bible days. It will be recalled that Jacob's children by the slaves of his two wives helped form the Twelve Tribes. Here at least is where the Moors score one, for after all there are no illegitimate children; there are only illegitimate parents.

Polygamy has this advantage over monogamy, as one Arab, who spoke considerable French, told me. When a man has one wife, he said, she quarrels with him; when he has many, they quarrel among themselves. Besides, he said, Arabs do not eat with their wives—woman does not eat with man; nor father with son, among the orthodox, which includes the majority. The more orthodox the Moor, the more he secludes the woman.

There is considerable intrigue in the harems, I understand, and when a red slipper is at the door it signifies that wifey has a female visitor (who knows?) and that the husband must keep out. Nor dare the husband look over the roof. In a land where the roofs are very low to do so is almost unforgiveable an offense as for a Negro trying to vote in a democratic primary in Texas. But let the intriguing male beware; some morning, if he awakes at all, it will be with a yataghan, or Turkish dagger, in his back.

Girls marry at twelve, which is not so bad for Morocco, when one recalls that that is the age of consent in Virginia. Ben Tillman had it fixed at 14 in South Carolina, for, as he once said in a letter to the Maryland Suffrage News, Colored girls "would invariably take advantage of White men and boys who had sexual intercourse with them."

Mothers of the poor carry their babies tied to their backs like Indians. And there are plenty of children, a large number of them with head sores and sore eyes. I saw a mother on the streets carrying three, one strapped to her back, another seated on her shoulders, while she nursed the third as she walked along.

The styles would hardly please American ladies. They are as I described them before, and have not changed in a thousand years. Sex appeal in dress is absolutely non-existent; the Sumners and the Comstockians would certainly find themselves out of a job here so far as dress is concerned. All that one sees of the lady are her kohl-stained eye lids and crimsoned heels, minus stockings.

(Continued next week. Next week Mr. Rogers tells of slavery, religion, education and other interesting facts he personally observed in North Africa.)

WORDS "AMERICAN NEGRO" UNKNOWN TO ARABS, SAYS J. A. ROGERS

Writer Says Rich Moors Thought Him "Indian"—"English Officer;" Didn't Understand Word "Colored"

Invited To Live In Morocco; Sees Jews Darker Than Negroes; "Religion Holding People Back;" Hits "Fundamentalists" Here

The Pittsburgh Courier
April 16, 1927
J. A. Rogers

Continuing his article on Rabat, Morocco, French North Africa, Mr. Rogers writes:

On every hand I hear that slavery, domestic slavery, still exists in spite of the fact that the French prohibited sale in the market place when it took over Morocco some time in 1906. I recall reading of a former American Consul here who said it was his duty once to free four slaves—two White two Black—the property of a deceased American, who had turned Mohammedan, I am told that it is quite different from what American slavery was, and that many of the poor welcome it just as the English, German, French and Hollanders used to sell themselves into servitude in the American colonies to escape privations at home.

Religion

Life centers around the Koran, and to this fact must be attributed largely the backwardness and the great poverty of the people, for Morocco is a land rich in grain, hides and minerals. Here is a book, part written, part compiled by Mohamet nearly fifteen hundred years ago, and yet in spite of changing conditions, in spite of outside pressure, it still dictates the daily life—a great weapon of the rich against the poor. The average Moor is very religious, very dirty, very hospitable, very superstitious. Just as in the days of the Arabian Nights there is the great fear of Dijuns, or evil spirits. It is said that they will not plough the soil very deep lest one turns up a djinoon, who makes his home there. In Morocco one realizes the perfect truth of Karl Marx's saying: "Religion is the opium of the people."

It happens to be the Moslem religion this time, but let not the Christians forget that Europe was in a similar plight when all life centered around the Bible, and this at a time when the Moslems were a powerful figure in Europe, Asia, and Africa. It is science's mastery over matter, together with the propelling force of gunpowder that has taken Christianity over the world and has made it supreme today. One of the surest means of reducing America, with all its splendid comforts and conveniences, to the final level of Morocco and the East would be to let the anti-evolutionists and the opposers of science which swarm in darkest America—the South—have their way. I shall never forget the sight of a little Colored preacher I heard in America denouncing science to his flock by the aid of electric light and in a church built by scientific methods.

The psychologic effects of all religions, no matter which, is the same, and when used for any other purpose except that of building up a spirit of brotherhood among all men, is that of dope, paralyzing effort as one sees it here, and replacing action with the wish and the hallucination.

Of course, seeing all this here is to me novel and interesting, and perhaps I really do not wish to change it any more than White people who go slumming in Harlem and other Negro districts would like to see the disappearance of Jim Crow sections, with all the Negroes well educated. It would be too much like myself and all the "kick" would be gone. For instance, the thrill and weirdness of hearing the muezzin, which even as I am writing this is calling to prayer with its long-drawn chant: "Lah Allah, il Allah! Allah Mohammed Rasoul Allah!" (There is no God but God, and Mohammed is His prophet!).

Education

The education of the children among the poor is confined almost solely to the reciting of passages from the Koran, and they may be heard in their tiny schools—a little room—droning it like bees, or may be seen squatting in the centre of a crowd in a square—a great, dirty crowd, the blind, the lame, the deformed, the eaten with disease, while some elderly man, white, black or yellow, with a finger drum, is chanting, evidently something religious from the signs that are being made and the gravity of the faces. Some of the rich Arabs send their children to the best schools in Europe, and as was said, Fez is a great centre of learning.

Churches

Infidels, which in this case, includes Christians, are not permitted in the churches as I soon discovered when I ventured too closely to the door of one. This happened to be shortly after one o'clock, and as I stood at the door I could see each arrival take off his sandals at the door, shake the dust out, and walk in where from the corner of the screen I could see them prostrating themselves on prayer mats. There are no seats. This happens to be the period of Ramadan, and rich Moors, in luxurious motor cars, were arriving with the very poor. At the entrance on both sides was a host of forlorn and most piteous beggars.

From some of the methods of treating disease, it seems to me that this is no place for a modern doctor. The usual method among the poor is for the native doctor to write out a verse of the Koran, and place it on the afflicted part. If there is a cure it is Kismet, the will of God; if there is none, that also is Kismet. Quite simple! A sort of Christian science. For a pain in the chest the sick man is likely to get a severe wallop in that region. Heroic treatment with a vengeance. After Christians have had a good laugh at that let them take down White's "Warfare Between Science, Theology in Christendom" and read that Vesalius, the first physician to dissect the human body, was hounded to his death. Rather interesting was the remark of a devout White American who was with me. Seeing them at worship he said: "Those people aren't Christians. They're just animals." Which happened to be precisely what many of the Moslems think of us, too, so far as our religion is concerned.

Through an interpreter I had an interesting conversation with two wealthy Moorish merchants, one of which was a dark Negro and the other with strong Semetic features and almost as dark. Both wanted to know what I was. I told them to guess. One said I was an Indian; the other said an English officer. I told them I was known as an "American Negro" directly. On further explanation I told them I was "Colored." That was no nearer. The closest definition they could arrive at was "Christian." Both said Morocco is a rich country and that I should remain. The wages of the average French laborer here is much higher than in France, being about two dollars a day, with low cost of living—that of a native, about fifty cents.

One must not forget the camels. They are the original gum-shoe men. By the way, the Arabs believe that camels were once men who broke faith in Allah. They have soft, noiseless feet; cross, fretful dispositions—all wear wicker muzzles, and as to odor, one wonders why people should pick on the skunk. Aiding the camel are hosts of patient little donkeys, often full of sores, like their drivers.

The headquarters of the Senussayah, or Senussi, said to be the most powerful secret organization in the world, numbering between ten and twenty millions of Africans of all colors, is here in Morocco, I believe at a place called Jof. Allied with Senussi are the Aisawa and the Hamidsha, the other secret orders, a trinity that hopes to see Islam once more triumphant in Europe and the European driven out of Africa. The Moors hope to recover Spain some day. Morocco, it will be recalled, once figured prominently in the American press. There is the famous saying of Roosevelt: Perdicaris alive, or Raisuli dead." The former, a naturalized American, had been captured by Raisuli, the bandit, and chained for four years in the mountains. This was Roosevelt's ultimatum to the Sultan of Morocco, and Roosevelt got Perdicaris.

Prejudice Against Jews

The only race prejudice here, if one can call it that, is against the Jew. Generally speaking they live in a different quarter, which is called Mellah—I am not sure if that is the way it is spelled. Both Europeans and natives agree that the Jew is even dirtier than the Arab. Well, he certainly isn't any cleaner or less free from sores. The Jews, however, are among the leading merchants. The Jewish women go unveiled. White Jews are comparatively few, the majority being the color of a rather dark Negro.

The very dark Negroes—and some of them are very, very dark—are known as "Afric," which means they have come from further South. There is no ill-feeling against them on that account; that is left to White Americans and Caucasianized Negroes.

{Next week Mr. Rogers writes on Gibraltar and Southern Spain. Do not miss it. Remember, in this newspaper Mr. Rogers, by

special arrangement, gives a more detailed account of his travels than in any other newspaper carrying his articles. Follow him in THE PITTSBURGH COURIER only.}

ROGERS CLIMBS ROCK OF GIBRALTAR; HAS PRAISE FOR SPAIN

American Writer Says Moors Gave Spaniards Culture Which Still Dominates Their Lives

Many Races In One Noted In Natives of Gibraltar; Mentions Town Hall Where In 1906 European Powers Met and Divided Africa Among Themselves.

Pittsburgh Courier
April 23, 1927
J. A. Rogers

GIBRALTAR, Spain, Apr. 21.—To reach Gibraltar one travels northward through Spanish Morocco, arriving at the international town of Tangier. I would like to say something about the Moors under Spanish rule, but I fear enough has already been said about Morocco. This much might be said, however, the customs are pretty much the same, also the Moors seem worse off under Spanish rule than under French. Spain, whose history is closely wrapped up with Morocco, is also a decadent nation—a has-been. Of this I shall have more to say later. Tangier, as was said, is an international town, perhaps the only one in the world, and there is a great difference between its appearance and that of Cueta, under Spanish rule.

From Tangier, home of the famous tangerine oranges, one gets a fine view of Spain, across the strait, with Gibraltar at its extreme tip, rearing its head a thrilling, awe-inspiring mass of gray, fifteen hundred feet straight up over the deep-blue of the Mediterranean. To one accustomed, as I was, to the popular pictures of Gibraltar, the front view will be a surprise, as from there it is cone-shaped. For the well-known picture one must see it from the rear, where it faces Spain like a couchant lion, with tail extended—a significant symbol of British power.

As one approaches the Rock by water the more he is impressed with its singular appearance. Small wonder that the Ancients thought this formidable mountain a sign placed there by their God, or gods, to mark the limit of the world. Small wonder that in a superstitious age Columbus was thought a mad-man when he set sail to the westward of it.

And not only is Gibraltar unique in appearance, but in history also. This rock of 1,266 acres has been perhaps the most fought over bit of land on earth—the Achilles' heel of Spain, changing Spain's history and that of the world.

The first battle for its possession was fought in 711 A.D. when Jabal-Tarik, Moorish conqueror, from whom its name is derived, sailed across from Africa with his army, and captured it. Building a castle on the rock, Jabal-Tarik used it as a base from which he harassed Spain until he finally defeated the fair-haired Goths under their king, Roderick, at Andalusia, and annexed Spain. (See Southey's famous poem: "Roderick, the Last of the Goths.")

Thereafter the Spaniards made repeated attempts to capture the Rock, but the Moors held it for 748 years, when they were finally ousted from Spain, and driven back into Africa. This Negroid people gave to Spain, according to Draper and Buckle, great English historians, and Nietzsche, German philosopher, the finest culture it has ever had. They built the Alhambra, and profoundly influenced European civilization. Today the style of Moorish architecture dominates Spain, the houses, patios, courtyards, and ornamentation, both in Gibraltar and the parts of Spain that I have seen bearing a striking resemblance to those in Morocco.

Among the most famous of the Kings of Spain was Yakub- El Mansur, who had a regiment of cavalry, composed entirely of Sudanese, being the crack regiment or 10th Cavalry of its day. These Moors were and are of every shade between black and white. The Spanish, once fair-haired Germanic people, are now on the whole a brunette race, many Spaniards being the color of dark Mulattoes, a fact also due to Moorish influence.

And here, by the way, is a fact that gives the lie direct to the Lothron Stoddards, the Coxes, Powells, and others, who say that a mixture of races brings decay. Less than a century after the defeat of the Moors, Spain was the leading power in Europe. Charles V, of Spain, ruled all of Western Europe, except the British Isles, from Holland to Gibraltar.

The next struggle for Gibraltar was between England and Spain after the former had wrested mastery of the seas, following the defeat of the Spanish Armada. The British captured the Rock in 1704, and have held it ever since, despite a three-year siege by the Spaniards, who gallantly attempted to scale the face of the Rock. This was, indeed, a quixotic adventure, as the Rock was tunneled from the interior and batteries of cannons planted within. Today, from below, one sees blackened holes, tier on tier, hundreds of feet above, from which flashed sure death on all who dared approach from the open, unprotected country below. The guns, now all obsolete, are still there, and with permission of the Admiralty, and accompanied by a guide, one comes upon them after stumbling and climbing through what appears miles and miles of dark tunnels.

Verily, tunneling this solid rock was a Herculean task, but it was worth the price. To the Moors it meant their hold on Europe; to England, that also, and mastery of the Mediterranean. But today possession of the Rock is largely romance.

As the advent of gunpowder and the bullet made the armor of the knight almost useless, so the advent of the airship has already largely destroyed the value of Gibraltar as a key to the Mediterranean. If one climbs in the direction of the face of the Rock he will get a glimpse of huge modern cannon pointing Afric-wards—the whole being a clear target for the aeroplane. Nevertheless, as the guide pointed out, the Rock has tremendous strategic importance. It is used as a naval base, from which ships and supplies can rapidly be sent to Africa and the Orient. Many warships are in the harbor. I counted sixty, and stopped.

Town Kept Clean

Under the administration of the Admiralty, the town (for it has several thousands of inhabitants) is kept almost spotlessly clean, reminding one of the home of a very tidy housekeeper. What a difference when one crosses the flat stretch of neutral territory into Spain! The streets are swarming with people, and in the afternoon when the sailors and soldiers are off duty, one moves on the narrow main street with difficulty. Plenty of saloons, full of people drinking not near, but real beer, not to speak of pre-war Scotch and other drinks, reminding one of the good old U. S. A. in the year 1917 B. V. D. (Before the Volstead Disaster.)

Gibraltar, as one can guess, is a very hilly town and one needs a strong backbone and lungs. The climate is most delightful and the children and younger women ruddy with health. The soil also seems remarkably fertile from the huge cabbages in the garden. It is March, but the gardens are in full bloom.

Many Races In One

As to racial composition, it is about as motley as is to be found anywhere else—English, Spanish, Moroccan, Arab,

Levantine, Maltese, Algerian, Turkish, Hindu. There is also the famous "Rock Scorpion"—the native of Gibraltar—which is a mixture of almost every race on earth and is proud of it. Almost all the stores carry two sets of signs—Spanish and English. There is an astonishing flow of traffic between Gibraltar and the nearest Spanish town—La Linea—less than a mile away. Between La Linea and Gibraltar is a bit of empty land, belonging to no one, but should one there claim it, I suspect he would not find it so ownerless. This land separates the British and Spanish custom houses.

Needless to say there is no evidence of the "color line" and one is free to go anywhere in public places that money can take him. The cost of living is reasonable for an American, being a third less than in New York City. A good room can be had for sixteen shillings (four dollars) weekly, and an excellent meal worth a dollar or more in America for sixty cents. Wages are much lower than in America. Beer is fours cents, and wine eight. Both English and Spanish money (pesetas) are currency.

From the rear face of the Rock is a delightful pathway, skirting the side, from which one gets a splendid view of the Mediterranean, with many sailing fishing villages on its broad blue expanse. Walking for nearly a mile on the British side one comes to the stony little fishing village of Catalan, a delightful little place, reminding one of a picture he has seen somewhere. I understand the Spanish hope to recover the Rock some day.

From Gibraltar I crossed over into Spain, and as was said, there was a vast difference in appearance. Beggars swarmed on one from all sides. The narrow stony streets, with their lines of quaint houses, the old churches which abounded, with their fine paintings, the lotteries in full swing, the policemen in their stiff black caps and colorful costumes, wine shops swarming with peasants strumming their guitars, were, nevertheless, all picturesque. Still, one feels that his nation—mistress of her day—that once owned much of the Old World and almost all of the new, is a back number.

In La Linea is a plaza de torro—(bull ring) where bull fights are held every other Sunday. I had hoped to be able to describe one, but would have had to wait a week. A guide, however, took me through and described the manner in which the fights are staged.

Several miles away is the larger and better kept town of Algeciras, but bearing, nevertheless, a look, if not exactly of poverty, one in which prosperity is lacking. Algeciras will be of special interest to Colored people because it was in the little town hall here, that the powers of Europe met in 1906 and partitioned Africa among themselves.

In Spain also, or at least the part of it I saw, "the color line" was quite noticeable by its absence. The Spaniards with whom I came in contact were most courteous and kind.

(Next week Mr. Rogers moves on to Italy, and will write of the beautiful island of Sicily, in whose ancient culture, Ethiopia played so great a part. Don't miss it.)

ETHIOPIA AND EGYPT MADE NORDIC CIVILIZATION POSSIBLE

J. A. Rogers Writes Of Mediterranean Coast And Visits Island Of Sicily

American Observer Says Nordics Are Only Whites Naturally Inflicted With Color Prejudice.

Pittsburgh Courier
April 30, 1927
J. A. Rogers

Palermo, Sicily, April 21—When one recalls the tremendous part that the Mediterranean Sea has played in the history of mankind, it is with quite a thrill that he sees the ship on which he is a passenger steam out of the port of Gibraltar, past the British fleet, with its flashing signals, and turning its prow eastward through the dark waters of the Strait. It is night, and peremptory signals flash from the Rock demanding the name of the vessel and whither bound. Answering flashes, and the vessel proceeds on its way. This proceeding now is merely a rite. The submarine has changed all that. The German submarines that sank so many vessels in the Mediterranean discarded the little formality.

To the south under the bright semi-tropic starlight, is the low coast line of Africa, with its long beads of light; northward are the dark hills of Spain, with the Rock standing a veritable Goliath among them.

Yes, it is historic territory, this—territory which people known in our day as Negroes, so far back as history goes, played the initial part. Take away the part that they played, and the effect would be that of removing the foundation of a building. It was ancient Ethiopia and then Egypt that made European civilization possible.

It was from this coast to the south that those whom we call Negroes spread themselves all over Europe, Asia and Australia at a time when nations now in power were undreamt of, just as the White variety of mankind has spread over the world from Western Europe.

The shores along the Mediterranean are a veritable cemetery of master nations—Ancient Ethiopia, Egypt, Phoenicia, Greece, Rome, Carthage, Crete, Ottoman Empire, Venice, Naples, Morocco, Spain. The chief asset of these nations today are their ruins, and the tourists they attract. Can the dominating, exploiting masters of today expect a better fate?

It was among these shores, too, that the first chapter in the history of the Negro in the Western World was written. It was to Spain in 1442 that Antam Gonsalves, lieutenant of Prince Henry the Navigator, brought the first slaves from the coast of Guinea, and thence to the New World by Ovando half a century later.

It is also in this inland sea that is found the island of Delos, the greatest slave market of all time in which mankind of every color was sold. After the capture of Jerusalem, Titus brought captive Jews by the tens of thousands for sale there.

With glimpses now of the African, now of the European coast, one wakes up on the morning of the third day to see overawing mountains frowning down on the smiling town of Palermo in its snug little harbor.

Sicily! From long reading of Nordic literature, what is the first picture that arises in my mind? This: a saturnine individual, almost dark as a Negro, with a gleaming stiletto ready to plunge in your back if you but smile at his girl. Again, that of a bandit laying in wait for you behind a mountain crag. Going ashore, one finds that the only bandits are the boatmen who take you from the ship, and the usual ones to be found in America, the cabmen. Again, instead of being jealous about the lady Sicilians, one finds an obliging gentleman most eager to show him "the sights of the town."

One's first impression on landing is that he is back in an English-speaking country. The cabmen, boatmen, sellers of postcards, and what-not, the "pilots" all speak English even the beggars in Italy speak English. But just wait until you have touched the first street. Then you'd find that your English will be as useful as so much Dutch.

Now one has to rely on signs with thc hands for what he wants, and he really learns the all importance of language, and realize what a trick nature has played on man with so many differing tongues. Well, to make a long story short, to be in the company of a people whose language one does not know is just as good as being dumb. One's talk is just as intelligible as the throaty noises of a dumb man.

But money talks! One, however, is likely to find it a very partial interpreter with the odds against him. What better sucker ever came on the scene when the word stranger is written all over me. I order a cup of coffee with a roll minus butter, that one could buy in a similar place in New York City for 10 cents. I want to know how much, and make a sign like writing to the waiter. He shows me the figure 7. That means 7 lira, or nearly 35 cents. A native would have gotten it for 5 cents, but how can I protest? So thankful to escape with my pocketbook, I give him another lira for macaroni (tip) and make my exit. Yes, after all, Nordic literature is not wholly wrong: there are bandits in Sicily.

One's first impression of Palermo is that it is a dirty city that hangs it laundry and washed rags in front of its home to dry. But this is wrong. Walk on towards the mountains and he will find a modern city, well laid out with thriving shops, banks and arcades, swarming with well-dressed people. Further back are palatial homes with fine gardens. Palermo is a case of very old city becoming modernized.

Sicily is noted for its splendid climate. It is the Florida of Italy, where the rich make their winter homes. The gardens are in full bloom, and the last of the ripened oranges are on the trees.

In the old part of the city, with its narrow winding streets, with clothing strung straight across, live the poorer population, which seems to be in great numbers. Wages are perhaps a third of what it is in America, with the cost of living disproportionately high. Eggs are about 3 cents each, and oranges, rather small ones, two for a nickel. The markets have plenty of octopus, which seem to be the favorite dish of the poor, next to spaghetti, which may be seen drying on the lines almost everywhere.

Churches abound, with almost one on every corner. So are shrines on street corners and in business places—a picture of Christ or the Virgin Mary with an electric light burning in front of it. Formerly it was candles; so even science has its uses in religion.

Some of the churches are very old, with very fine paintings and carvings. There is a splendid cathedral built by the Christians in the Ninth Century. When the Arabs, who, as was said, are Negroid people, conquered Sicily, they turned the building into a mosque. When the Christians came back into power they turned the mosques into churches, one of which, San Giovanni degli Eremiti, is a fine example of Moorish art. The Normans also held the island at the time of the Crusades, and they, too, have left a fine example of their art in the Church of La Martorana.

On the heights, four miles above the city, is the Cathedral of Monreale, one of the best known in Europe.

Perhaps of all forms of education, travel is the most effective. For the one who is proud of his knowledge, and is at the same time capable of being cured, there is nothing else I know of that will make him realize how very little he does know, after all, of the sum of possible knowledge.

Here in Palermo I saw a sight that in my wildest dreams, aye, nightmares, I had never believed possible. And that is in the Capuchin Catacombs, where there are 8,000 human skeletons, row on row, some lying, the majority lined up, standing on shelves, clad in the same clothes in which they had been interred, some of them over 300 years ago. With grinning faces, some with the dried flesh still on their faces and bodies, and expressions so grotesque and weird that it is beyond the power of words to describe, they stand in all manner of poses, seeming to converse in a silent, ghastly language all their own. An unforgettable sight! Few of the women in the party could stand the sight, and the guide shortened the visit, to the regret of myself and several others.

All these mummies bear their names on a placard suspended in front of them. The oldest one bears the date 1662, the last 1882. All the unmarried women wear crowns, while the married ones go bareheaded, or rather bare-skulled. In those days the unmarried woman was considered unfortunate.

In color the Sicilians range from that of a dark Mulatto to blonde. As was said, the Arabs once conquered the island, leaving in addition to their civilization a great deal of their blood. There is no color line of any kind. The hotel keepers, restaurateurs, and others are too much interested in your coin for that. More and more I am seeing with my own eyes a theory I have always held—namely, that it is only English-speaking Nordics who are afflicted with the rabies of color hate. Just what kind of people Sicilians do not like, I haven't been able to discover yet. There are quite a few real Negroes who are here from Tripoli and Italian Africa, as well as from Abyssinia, but I have been unable to converse with any of them.

The island is also rich in specimens of Greek architecture. The Greeks were also among its owners. At the southern end is the city of Syracuse, which will be of particular interest to Christians because here was built one of the seven churches. It was not very far from there, off the coast of Malta, that St. Paul was wrecked. On the island is the active volcano Mt. Etna; while nearby on an adjoining island is Stromboli. Between Sicily and the mainland in the Straits of Messina is a whirlpool, which figured in Greek mythology as Scylla or Charybdis, I do not recall which. [Editor's Note: It was confirmed that the whirlpool was equated with Charybdis.]

In my next I will tell of Naples, and of my visit to Pompeii, the buried city and of the trip into the center of Mt. Vesuvius.

"I FIND ITALY A LAND OF ART"
–Writes J. A. Rogers
Courier Correspondent Visits Ancient Pompeii; Climbs Top Of Vesuvius, Sees Boiling Crater

Pittsburgh Courier
May 14, 1927
J. A. Rogers

NAPLES, Italy, May 5.—Naples, a city of unsurpassed natural beauty, reminds me of drunken Christopher Sly in Shakespeare's "Taming of the Shrew." Sly is kicked out of the alehouse, and while he is snoring in the snow, the Duke happens along, picks him up and places him, dirty clothes and all, in a magnificent bed in the castle.

Such is Naples which I will say without an instant's hesitation, is the dirtiest, most ill-smelling place I have ever been in. Bad as the poorer Moors were they at least kept their quarter swept, and besides had the advantage of having one-story houses with plenty of sunshine in the streets.

But in Naples the houses were built in the Middle Ages, tall permanent structures of stone with such narrow winding streets that one can often touch both sides with extended arms. Down these narrow shafts the sunlight strikes only at midday.

My first night in Naples I shall not easily forget. I was taken by an Italian who had been in America to a hotel (albergo, it is called here) run by his friend. It was a most primitive place but the proprietor, a very chich fellow, with flashing diamonds charged me the equivalent of a dollar, evidently prompted by my, or rather his friend. The same could be had in America for a third of the sum.

The room was not a pleasant smelling one to say the least, and I hurriedly threw open the window, since I had decided to stick it out and see some of the life one does not see at the better places. Rather tired, I soon fell asleep, but was awakened toward morning by a fearful odor, which came from the outside this time—the morning odor of Naples. Now I found myself faced with the alternative of the odor within and that without, and gladly chose the former. The next night I found a good hotel for which I would have had to pay, about the price I would in the South, but again towards morning the terrible odor forced me to close the window.

And the poverty and the beggars, which landed on us like Jersey mosquitoes at the pier! So piteous are they, that one must have a heart of stone to refuse some of them. If one were to give to half of the calls for aid he'd be a beggar himself in short order. One can see them and other unfortunates, swarming on the steps of the numerous churches, or forlorn figures within splendid cathedrals, their lips rapidly uttering prayers that are never answered. Their God is certainly asleep on the job, and one thinks of Elijah on Mount Carmel when he mocked the priests of Baal, telling them to pray louder as their God may be asleep or gone on a journey. Yet, in a world where some have so much and others nothing, religion seems to be the only opiate for the pain of this refuse of humanity. One wonders how some do exist from day to day. The beggars in Naples are no better off than in Morocco. Besides the African poor had sunlight and knew how to smile. These are woebegone, too desolate for words.

An unpleasant picture, but that is by no means all of Naples. Down towards the bay, the most beautiful I have ever seen, are fine modern mansions, with even more palatial ones going up. There is the beautiful Castel Nuovo, the Royal Palace in a commanding position on one of the many hills in the city, the Porta Capuana, and the Riviera di Chaia and the Via Caracciolo, majestic promenades.

And the odor is not the only thing that strikes one at night. There are the serenaders with their stringed instruments on the streets. I heard a group of five boys, the oldest not over 12, singing, and I cannot recall ever having heard better voices and finer feeling put into song. And the manner in which each one could play a tambourine, would have brought them all a fat salary on the American stage.

Italy is indeed the land of art, and of this I shall have much to say later.

Get out of the city and one is immediately in the land of enchantment. In the distance is Mount Vesuvius, its crater like a great scooped out hole, with the little Vesuvius and majestic Mount Pompano overlooking the bay, while dim in the blue haze lies the towering Island of Capri with its famous Blue Grotto. All around one on the train bound for Pompeii, are beautiful gardens, olive groves and orange orchards flaming with yellow fruit. Spring and autumn joining hands. Now and then one sees a column, relic of old Roman civilization.

An hour and a half, and one is at Pompeii, the entrance fee to which is about 36 cent. And here a bit of advice to prospective visitors. Shun the numerous guides—one of the biggest pests imaginable—and who after agreeing on a fixed price will try to bleed you for all you are worth. And whatever you do, don't try to argue with them, for even if you are a woman, here is one instance in which you will never get the last word. Either get a guide book and see the city yourself or take a tour with one of the reliable agencies. A Baedeker will serve for all practical purposes.

Pompeii is another unforgettable site. Life played a cruel joke on these Romans of 79 A. D. for the benefit of posterity. One fine night, Vesuvius, which is about ten miles away as the crow flies, spouted forth a deluge of flaming ashes, covering the city as Mont Pelee did in Martinique, embalming inhabitants and their customs for present day instruction as no book is capable of doing. For a description of this awful event read Lytton's "Last Days of Pompeii." Here are the streets, the wine-shops, baths, the palaces, temples, apartment buildings, tribunals, fountains, houses of prostitution, just as the people fled from them minus the tops which were removed by the excavators.

Among the most interesting sights there are: the vomitorium, where these old Romans would go to have the doctor relieve them of the food they had just eaten in order that they might start in feasting afresh; the ruins of a home with the mosaic of a chained dog at the gateway with the sign: Cave Canem (beware of the dog); the Turkish baths and the dancing halls with their lewd pictures painted on the wall; the prisons; a remarkable marble fountain bearing the cost of erection, equivalent to ten dollars but which would cost several hundred times that today; the museum, with many of the inhabitants transfixed into hard lime in the exact pose in which death overtook them; the treasures and the objects of household use, together with bread and grain incinerated by the fire, and even the little dogs. And one must not forget the Domus Vettiorum (House of Vetti). Vetti was a general provider of humanity, everything from soup to nuts. Ladies today are not permitted into a certain part of his establishment which makes them all the more curious, and they may be seen peering in on us members of the more fortunate sex, from the outside, eager, if not permitted to see, at least to hear. The least that can be said of these old Romans was that they were certainly frank, and if our newspapers today are in such a mental state over the pictures of nude human beings, it is difficult to imagine what sort of straight-jacket would be necessary for the editors could they suddenly be transported to those days with their indescribable signs striking the eyes not only on the sides of the houses, but carved in stone on the sidewalk.

The city had a remarkably fine site with majestic Mount Pompano to the east and the extraordinarily beautiful Bay of Naples in front. Another city, Herculaneum, met a similar fate at the time, but that is a less popular sight.

Leaving Pompeii with regret, and the guide, if you have had one, with great pleasure—if you have the general run of luck you'll find it as difficult to leave him as it was to get rid of him when you started out—one stops at Pugliano for the trip to the top of Mt. Vesuvius, which by tram and funicular railway up, up the mountain is four thousand feet up above the city. On the way up one passes great areas of black lava, the whole appearing as if some enormous plough had gone over the land, making very deep furrows. One sees also the remains of dwellings and towns of different periods rebuilt by the bolder ones after each eruption. There are still many houses on the sides of the mountain, many of which were destroyed in the recent eruption. And others are re-building. Hope, indeed, springs eternal in the human breast. Besides, the land is very fertile.

Descending to the very edge of the crater one gets glimpses of its black bosom between the columns of smoke coming out from invisible fissures, while an enormous black wall rears itself high above one, verily a pit such as only the genius of a Homer or Dante is capable of describing. One hears also the deep rumble from the depths of the mountain, and the lava bubbling and boiling within, all ready at its fancy to begin hurling red-hot rocks hundreds of feet in the air. A government observatory on the mountain takes constant record of its pulse, and warns the people below when it is about to have another eruption.

By rail is quite expensive. There is another by auto and horse back which serves the same purpose. In any case the service of a government guide into the crater is compulsory. And the view from the mountain top! That alone is almost worth the price.

There are many interesting customs here, and of these together with the general life of the people I will say more when I shall have seen more of Italy. One thing I have discovered is that there is little love lost between the Northern Italian and the Southern one, and one gets as ready a hearing from the former against the latter as a Northern White man will get from a Southerner when it is a case of the Negro; or that a Negro will get from a White Californian against the Japanese. Jews also are very little liked.

My French I have found indispensable as most of the educated classes seem to speak it. Whenever I wish to find my way all that is necessary is to approach one of the numerous priests in their long, flowing black garb. All speak French.

In my next I will write of Rome. A part of this article was written there, and it is even more wonderful than I had imagined.

ROGERS IN ROME: CALLS IT "ETERNAL CITY"
Writer Overwhelmed At Sight Of St. Peter's, "Largest Christian Church In World"
Says Articles, From This On, Will Deal Less With Race Problem As Negroes There Live As Whites, According to Their Means

Pittsburgh Courier
May 21, 1927
J. A. Rogers

ROME, ITALY, May 19.—Rome, the Eternal City! Rome, that from her seat on the Seven Hills, ruled the then known world!

Rome, of whom were one citizen, he, White, or Black, became automatically an aristocrat!

The Coliseum; the Baths of Caracalla; the Palaces of the Caesars; the Capitol, in which Julius Caesar, Pompey, Brutus, Cicero once moved as living personages; the Temple of Venus; Rome, the foundation and capital of Christianity, aye, it will take a far abler pen than mine, or should I say typewriter, to do justice to the theme.

But before I attempt anything, let me relate a rather interesting incident that took place on the train in route from Naples.

In the compartment in which I was—first and second class on European trains are compartments—were five other persons, four Italians and a Frenchwoman. As it occurred all spoke French, and soon we were conversing. The Italians were all Fascists, and as I spoke well of Mussolini—indeed, I had better speak well of him—we became very friendly. Things went on like this for some time, until two Germans, a man and his wife, entered. Suddenly there was a frost. The effect was precisely the same as if the scene were in the South, my five friends, White Southerners, and the two Germans, Negroes. To me, with not a particle of ill-will against the Germans in particular, the strong dislike shown by my five friends, was as little comprehensible as it would have been to the five were they in the South, and the newcomers Negroes.

The Germans, sensing the attitude of the others, kept to themselves. The only remark made on their part was addressed to me, the man asked for the loan of a French newspaper that was on the table.

Intensely interested as I was in the situation, I was to become more so for by and by a young priest, a very pleasant, smiling, young fellow looked in at the door, and began to talk to the two Germans in German. I did not understand a word of what they were saying but the priest radiated such good nature, that I couldn't help smiling back at him, whereupon one of my Fascist friends lifted his newspaper to cover the side of his face and made an ugly face at me, as if "to put me wise" that it wasn't the proper thing to smile on Germans.

Later, the Germans left, and I was not at all surprised to hear one of the Fascists declare that that species of "cochon" (swine) oughtn't to be permitted to ride among decent people, while the lady, who also happens to be returning from Morocco, thanked heaven that the French government barred all Germans from its African territory.

Tempted as I am to draw a moral from this for folks at home, I will refrain and go on to tell of Rome.

Rising bright and early the next morning and thrilling

with the newness of it all, I started out to see the city. Shunning the numerous guides and drivers of horse-cabs who wanted to take me around, I decided to take pot-luck and stumble on the sights myself. So I wandered forth hoping first of all to see the Coliseum, but I didn't then, although it was on the same street as my hotel and quite nearby. Later I did stumble upon it and the thrill was all the greater.

Strolling on I passed fine gardens and magnificent homes—Rome is a very clean city, and in some parts quite modern. In a park I saw a White nurse leading along by either hand two little boys, one White, the other a dark Mulatto, dressed in a jaunty sailor suit and carrying a cane. It was clear that the children belonged to a good family, or families. I was anxious to learn something about them, but unfortunately none of the three spoke English or French.

Wandering down the Via Nazionale (National Street) one of the leading thoroughfares, I finally turned into a side street to find myself in one of those picturesque old quarters with its narrow winding streets and houses of stone, peculiar to Latin Europe. A few minutes later and I was in the Capitol, with its time-stained statutes, the most noticeable of which is that of one of the early Caesars, Marcus Aurelius, on horseback. What history has been enacted on this site! Here it was that Julius Caesar was murdered—a fate that even those who have difficulty with his commentaries will agree that he did not deserve.

Moving on I find myself in the Quirinal. What the Quirinal was all about I have forgotten now and those wishing to know more about it will have to look up their Roman history. [Editor's Note: Quirinal is one of the Seven Hills of Rome (the tallest), upon which was constructed a papal palace (Palazzo del Quirinale) in the 16th century where Italian Kings lived from 1870-1946. In addition to four Italian Kings, thirty popes and eleven presidents have also lived there.]

And just about here, it will be necessary to warn my readers that I am going to get, perforce, very far away from the color question in this and other articles, since there is simply none to write about. The few Negroes here live precisely as White people, that is, they go where their money takes them. Our tremendous race question in America seems to bear about the same relation here as a back fence quarrel does to a conference of diplomats. An American, White or Black, will find the best of everything wished on him, because he is supposed to be like the Treasury at Washington, bursting with gold.

To resume: near the Quirinal is the King's palace, a magnificent structure of marble, which is open to the public on certain days, while not far away is the monument to Victor Emmanuel II, and the Unknown Soldier, which is said to be the finest monument built in Europe in a century.

Wandering on I passed many arches and other relics of the old Romans, one of the most interesting of which was a part of the wall of old Rome, which now serves as a foundation for modern buildings.

My next thrill was on coming on a large, rapid river spanned by splendid bridges. At once I recognized the Tiber (Fiume Tevere, as it is called here), made famous by Shakespeare and across which Julius Caesar failed to swim. Going on, passing many peasants, and frequently stopped by guides and sellers of postcards, who feel that you ought to patronize them and tell you so—to a tourist it finally comes to seem that there cannot be less than nine-tenths of the population engaged in these lines—I arrive at the Castel San Angelo, a formidable looking fortress nearly 1800 years old and with several remarkable sieges to its credit. Over this castle, it is also said, the

Archangel Michael appeared in the act of sheathing his sword to Pope Gregory the Great in 590 A. D. to assure him that a pestilence then ravaging Rome would be stayed. One hears much of that sort of thing here. For instance, in a little church on the Appian Way, named Domine Quo Vadis, is a marble block with the imprint of two feet, in a manner so clumsy as I believe no human being would stand, much less a deity. These footprints, one is told, are those of Christ when he appeared to Peter as the latter was about to desert Rome. But perhaps more of this later.

Looking back from the Castel San Angelo I spy a magnificent dome, surmounted by a cross and a thrill tells me: "There is St. Peter." I start off in the direction but after half an hour's walk I find myself back at the Tiber. In Europe's winding streets one cannot steer straight as in America. I start again, and better luck this time. A few minutes and I come upon the Piazza or Square of St. Peter—a magnificent colonnade, broad, sweeping, with an obelisk in the center, and two great fountains spouting water high in the air. To give some idea of its size, the colonnade has two sweeps of 142 columns each ornamented by 192 statutes of saints, each 16 feet high.

Steering to the left to avoid the horde of guides and venders who are awaiting me, I arrive at the broad stone steps, which must be several hundred feet wide, and enter the cathedral to behold the most wonderful, most thrilling sight I have ever seen—like some wonderful vision, sweeping away the breath by sheer grandeur. I have seen some of the most magnificent creations of men and of Nature, but never anything like this. I simply shan't attempt a description of it, indeed, I believe that no genius that ever lived could do justice to St. Peter, for is it not the handiwork, itself, of the greatest geniuses of the human race—designers, sculptors, painters—for the past six hundred years? Use all the adjectives of wonder, magnificence, grandeur, beauty, and still none would be far away from conveying a scintilla of the praise due this cathedral, the largest Christian church in the world. Verily, the men who built this had something else on their brain beside the Charleston, the black bottom, the numbers, "Nigger Heaven," "Fine Clothes to the Jews," and the sort of degenerate or infantile stuff that White publishers in America would pin our Negro writers down to. St. Peter is a sight that at once humbles and exalts, and I could not help thinking how so many of us, wrapped in our petty conceits, and thinking we are alive, are really dead, so far as the finer, nobler things are concerned.

Byron wrote: "While the Coliseum stands, Rome stands." I hold no brief for Catholicism any more than I do for Protestantism, Shintoism [Editor's Note: Shinto is the indigenous spirituality of Japan], or any other religion, but I feel like saying in a similar vein: "While St. Peter stands, Catholicism stands." To this Temple of Beauty, hundreds of thousands make annual pilgrimages. As I remarked to a Scotch priest who came up and spoke to me: Even the Imperial Wizard himself couldn't help being carried away with it. Those old popes were patrons of art in the highest sense.

And as I look on, lost in admiration, I felt that my fellow Negroes were capable of doing nothing less had they but the vision and the ambition.

Among the noteworthy things within the Cathedral are the decorations of the great dome which is 450 feet over one's head; the Papal Altar; Michaelangelo's "Pieta" and the bronze statue of St. Peter, the right foot of which is worn smooth by the kisses of devotees in the last 1500 years. Your humble servant did not kiss it for more reasons than one; he was content to stand by and watch others in line doing so.

"ROMAN IDEA OF LIFE CAME FROM ETHIOPIANS" - J. A. ROGERS

New Yorker Gives Detailed Description Of Historical Ruins Seen On Study Tour

Says if U.S. Continues It Will Excel Vastness If Not Beauty of Famous and Renowned Pagan Empire

(Pittsburgh Courier's Editor's Note: Mr. Rogers writes the Editor he has received many letters from Courier readers concerning his trip, and will later devote a special article to answering questions asked by these inquiries. He will be glad to get further letters from persons interested in his trip. He may be addressed J. A. Rogers, 11 Rue Scribe, care American Express Company, Paris, France. Postage is five cents to Paris. His mail will be forwarded to him from there.)

Pittsburgh Courier
May 28, 1927
J. A. Rogers

ROME, ITALY, May 26.—To tell but few of the interesting things to be seen in this superb city would take several articles and so in this concluding one on Rome I shall have to touch but briefly on some of the highlights.

From the stand point of historical interest the chief place is undoubtedly what is known as the Foro Romano, an enclosed area of not less than a hundred acres in the heart of the city. Here is the spot around which once revolved the power that ruled the world, but now a place of fallen columns; masses of the mightiest masonry imaginable; and a few marble columns, standing forlornly here and there, held together by bands of steel.

There is an admission fee but I struck the Foro Romano on a Sunday afternoon free and wandered for hours over the same ground that Caesar Augustus, and Popaea, Brutus, Messalina, Cicera, St. Peter and St. Paul, and Septimus Severus, all trod. The latter, by the way, was undoubtedly of Negro ancestry, as his busts reveal.

Among the most interesting ruins here are the Roman Forum, where great debates were once waged; the Temple of Saturn, whose eight granite columns still stand; the Arch of Septimus Severus; the Rostra, or Tostrum, on which the orators mounted to address the people; the Temple of the Empress Faustina, with her name on the marble horizontal, still standing. Part of this was later turned into a Christian church, which still later formed part of the ruin. There are also the Temple of Castor and Pollux, from which if I mistake not, war used to be declared; the Temple of Janus, with its two faces, War and Peace, and from which later we got the word, Janus-faced, to designate hypocrites. Nearby are also the Vestal Virgins, who kept the sacred fires of Rome burning constantly for over a thousand years—it was with one of these vestal ladies that Julius Caesar first got himself in dutch; the Temple of the Empress Julia on the steps of which the body of Julius Caesar was cremated; while most remarkable of all are the mighty ruins of the Temple of Venus. Next to war, Love came first in the hearts of those old Pagans. Later a part of this Temple was turned into a Christian church, which still stands.

All this, by the way, is getting far away from the color question, still, I think, we writers usually misjudge the range of interest of the average Colored reader.

There are more than eight other Temples in this vicinity, but before passing on one must not forget to mention that near here was the old Jewish ghetto which lasted for more than 1900 years. The Jews, it will be recalled, were first brought as captives to Rome by Pompey, but in less than seventeen years had become a power in Rome, just as forty-five years after the Negro was brought to America, destitute, a law was passed in Virginia forbidding Negroes from buying White people. (See Hening's "Statutes of Virginia, Vol. I.")

Leaving this vicinity one climbs the Palatine, one of the famous Seven Hills, on which was built the Palaces of the Caesars.

The mighty masses of brick, minus their facings of costly marble still stands like imperishable cliffs. The Palaces of the Caesars! Need one say more to stir the mind to ideas of grandeur and magnificence. From this height one gets a splendid view of the city. Wandering on, one passes through what was once the Garden of the Caesars, at this time of the year with trees laden with ripe oranges, and arrives at another artificial cliff with arches so immense that later they served as churches for the Christians. Under these arches are still to be seen the paintings on the wall of the early Christians.

It is impossible to give an idea of the colossal size of these ruins. This fact strikes one, especially after he shall have seen the Coliseum, the Aqueducts, and the Baths of Caracalla: those old Romans built with a robustness, a vastness, far beyond us. They had a mightier conception of life. But, of course, it will be recalled that they inherited from the Egyptians, who in turn got their idea from the Ethiopians.

Still, in expressing the above idea, one must not forget to add that if the United States, and particularly New York City, continues as it has been doing, Americans will excel Rome in vastness of architecture, if not in beauty.

Near Palatine was where the Rape of Sabines took place. It will be recalled that when Romulus found Rome, there were no ladies, and the men got rather lonely. How to get some? Romulus invited the Sabines, a neighboring tribe, to see the games. They came, bringing their wives and daughters, and while all were absorbed in watching the races and wrestling, the Romans simply helped themselves.

Not far from the Palatine is the Coliseum, so vast and so changed by the march of Time, that it hardly seems to be the handiwork of man. It reminds one, especially at its top, of some of the strange cliffs one sees in the Great American Desert. In the great arena where men and beasts once came to death grips, and Christian martyrs were torn by lions, are children playing hopscotch, or parties of tourists gazing on. Near the place where once sat the Caesars, the pointing of whose thumbs meant death or life, are pigeons building their nests and wooing their mates.

The circumference of the Coliseum is almost half a mile, and took the labor of thirty thousand slaves. It seated eighty thousand. At its opening in 80 A. D. there was a performance that lasted one hundred days, during which thousands of men and wild animals tore each other to pieces. These games, it will be recalled, were put to an end by the act of Telemachus, an old man, who, horrified at the brutality, walked into the arena one night, stepped between battling gladiators and was killed—a deed that stirred the populace, then undergoing the leavening influence of Christianity.

Much of this Roman history of mine is faulty, for if there is one thing one learns here, it is how little he knows after all, indeed, that is the effect of travel in general.

Later the Coliseum was used as a fortress. This, in addition to the fact that much of its costly material was taken to build palaces elsewhere, accounts for its present appearance.

Not far from the Coliseum is the Circus Maximus, which is 737 yards long, 236 yards wide and held 300,000 persons, almost four times the capacity of the Coliseum. Read your Ben Hur and Quo Vadis if you want to live over again the exciting scenes that took place in this now deserted spot.

Another ruin nearby, hardly less massive than the Coliseum, and perhaps larger, are the Baths of Caracalla, begun by Septimus Severus. Here was one of the places where the Roman populace used to come in large numbers to bathe, an institution later discouraged by the Christians, who neglected their bodies and personal habits as the Romans had observed them. Much of the lack of bathing in Catholic Europe must be attributed to Christian influence. It seems that mankind is not too overfond of bathing, anyway, except in very hot countries.

This great bath accommodated more than a thousand persons at once, and the hot water pipes and the beautiful mosaics in what were once pools may still be seen. In the upper stories were libraries and art galleries. Among the art relics later found here were the Hermaphroditus, the Farnese Bull, and the torso of the Apollo Belvedere.

Leaving the Baths and going along the famed Appian Way, one arrives after a walk of two or three miles at the Catacombs of San Callisto. These catacombs were burying places, and cover some 32 acres underground, being in three stories, the first being 40 feet deep. Here, in these gloomy depths the Christians used to worship. Later, many of the early popes were buried here.

The tombs have nearly all been broken into—the act of the Vandals, when they descended on Rome, determined to wipe out her culture. The handiwork of these Nordics may be seen everywhere.

These Catacombs, one of many, are now under the care of the Trappist monks, one of whom with his shaven crown, sandals and flowing brown robe took us into the vaults. Unfortunately, I chose the English-speaking group and saw little. These were several Americans, belonging to a type of tourist who is frankly bored with everything and would much rather be in a cabaret, but dutifully visit every place in order to be able to say that they had been there. After they had seen a little of the first layer they asked to be taken out, and the guide complied.

While going down the Appian Way, I passed a party of young girls, the oldest not over twelve. There wasn't a bobbed haired one among them, nor any sign of rouge or lipstick, most of the women here have quite as ruddy a complexion as the Seventh Avenue belles with the difference that it doesn't cost those here anything. Still the girls I saw were setting a pace for our American girls: they were nearly all smoking cigarettes, giving one another a light just like boys. Dozens of persons were passing, but I seemed to have been the only one who was surprised.

Back in the vicinity of the Foro Romano is the historic Carcere Mamertino, or Mamertine Prison, where Nero caused both Paul and Peter to be imprisoned. Their cell was cold, damp and of solid stone underground, and no place for a tall man. Being in prison those days certainly wasn't a joke.

Nevertheless, it was these same two men, whose influences overthrew the power of Imperial Rome, and took the popes from their hiding place in the Catacombs to regal power in the Vatican. Peter's vision of a world empire ruled by Christianity had won.

Another important place is the Vatican library with what must be miles and miles of art treasures. In this building is the famed Sistine Chapel, painted by Michaelangelo, which is always thronged with visitors, as well as one painted by Raphael; the Royal Room built by Paul III, reigning Pope; the Borgia Apartment, thousands of books with signatures sent from all parts of the world to the Popes, one of which bears the names of 33,000 French persons who declare they "are ready to suffer and die for the faith;" Nero's bath; the Apollo Belvedere, and the Egyptian Room with some of the finest specimens of Egyptian art yet discovered.

One could speak of other places as the Church of San Stefano reared by Pope Leo I presented to the Ethiopians in 450 A. D.; the tombs of Shelley and Keats in the Protestant cemetery; the American Academy; the Pantheon; the Doria Palace; the Villa Borghese, of Frascati, with its beautiful villas, and the home of Cicero; of the Rocca di Papa, or Pope's Rock, which it is said was about to fall when a peasant seeing the danger prayed to the Virgin, who apparently being reminded of her duty, of protecting the faithful, stayed its fall, but there seems no end to the interesting places one could mention in Rome.

If ancient Rome ruled the world by sword modern Rome rules by the might of beauty, for while these treasures are here the eyes of all lovers of beauty will be turned towards her.

"Negroes are learning that progress is made not from ideas, but from the practical application of ideas." -George B. Blount.

ROGERS IN MONTE CARLO; CALLS IT "NUMBERS PARADISE"
Writer From Harlem Plays 100 Francs At Casino And Loses; No Color Line There

---

Tells How Church Winks At Gambling; Dollars Only Requirement to Get Anything Wanted

Pittsburgh Courier
June 4, 1927
J. A. Rogers

[Pittsburgh Courier's Editor's Note—In a letter to the Editor, Mr. Rogers says he is having an interesting time and is preparing some special interviews with leading figures of Europe for readers of the Courier. He says: "The people here are very much interested in the Negro in America; indeed, everywhere I go. Saturday I had an interview with Deputy Delmont, one of the biggest men in France, and he promised to put me in touch with the Minister of the French Colonies and other big folk. Have many interesting articles ahead for you. For instance, I was in Marseilles, the city with the greatest Colored population in Europe; also I have been meeting quite a few of the distinguished Negroes here." As we told Courier readers in the beginning, Mr. Rogers is writing a more detailed story of his travels for The Courier than any other paper in which his articles appear. Those wishing to write him may do so at 11 Rue Scribe, care of the American Express, Paris, France. Postage 5 cents.

MONTE CARLO, June 2.—Emerson said something to the effect that the one who could do any given thing better than his fellows, though he lived in the woods, would find a path beaten to his door by the world. The same may be said about climate: Give any part of the world an exceptional climate, and no matter what the other features are, you'll find the roads of the world leading there.

This at least is the thought that strikes me on seeing

the famed Cote d'Azure (the Azure coast). Rocks! Rocks! And then ever so many rocks! Overawing mountains, great precipices, mountain sides so steep that they seem more fit for goats than men; yet try to buy some of that rock, particularly around Monte Carlo, and you'll think you are bargaining for oil land. This is the most fashionable spot on earth, the playground of everyone Who is Who the world over.

Monte Carlo is in Monaco, which latter is an independent principality only eight square miles in extent, a little over 5,000 acres of rock all told, and yet perhaps more real wealth is to be found here than in many other European countries put together. Society with a capital "S" is here. Wealth drifts here, as fat boils to the top of a pot. At a charity affair given here a few days ago there were three reigning kings, and an equal number of queens, princesses, dukes, counts and others galore, not to speak of American multi-millionaires. In the harbors of Monaco and Cannes I counted 22 yachts that had come from ports in America alone, and as far South as Palm Beach.

And this wealth has been used to transform these rocks into perhaps the most lovely spot on Earth, for Monte Carlo, together with the town of Monaco, make the fairyland you have always read about but never seen. As I wander through it, seeing the town and other things I shan't mention yet, I find myself laughing at myself. Here I had been all these many years fancying myself really alive!

And I couldn't help thinking the same, too, of certain other very important folk I know, not all of whom, by the way, are of the pink-skinned persuasion.

I have said that it is the climate that is the magnet. But do all these folk to whom excitement is the very breath of their existence flock here because of the caress of the delightful air, the bathing, the yachting? Well, now, do not the younger generation of Negroes go to church expressly for the service; that young lady who accosted me yesterday in Nice—didn't she do so because I am so handsome and she simply couldn't resist my sex appeal, and a hundred other things that look just so.

Of course there is a Casino, but that only happens to be here.

The Casino

Monaco is perhaps the only country of its kind in the world. No one pays taxes of any kind here. But how is its marvelous beauty kept up, its great sea-walls and bridges built, its fine roads, its orchestra, delightful walks, oceanographic museum, incomparably beautiful lawns and gardens all maintained? Besides, has not Monaco a royal family of its own? And a royal family, as everyone knows, takes money to run. Why, it would seem that these 4,000 or so souls on this barren bit of rock would be about as hard pressed doing this alone as many of us in keeping a car running, or paying the installments on the piano. Yes, one can't see how it is done, but it's done. The secret? Ah, the Casino! "The strength of Monaco is the weakness of the world."

The Casino pays to the principality something like five million dollars a year for the concession, and is run by a company bearing the quite innocent name of "Sea Bathing Association." So the good pious folk of Monaco—for there is a cathedral—as a return for keeping quiet about the Casino, pay no taxes. Besides, consider the high price of land caused by the presence of the Casino. Now all the good folk on the other side of the Atlantic who wouldn't tolerate gambling under those conditions, please hold up your hands.

One thing, however, is absolutely forbidden. A Monegasque (native of Monaco) must not enter the Casino. Like the hootch vendor too wise to touch his own stuff, Monaco reserves that for the foreigner—it's perfectly good enough for them.

The history of Monaco dates back to the days of Grecian mythology. Hercules is said to have performed one of his labors here—was it the killing of some bull? I have forgotten. Later the Ethiopians, Phoenicians and others used it as a harbor. But what I want to call attention to is the fact that not so long ago the Monegasque were pirates. Today the sword has been laid aside—not exactly beaten into ploughshares, since there is no land to till. In its place there is a little wooden rake, which is quite as effective.

A Visit to the Casino

The Casino resembles one of those fancy buildings one sees at Coney Island or other amusement parks, except that it is much more beautiful, more solidly built. In front is one of the most beautiful gardens I have ever seen, while from the rear is a sea view quite as remarkable.

Going up the steps, I entered the palatial building and, seeing others walking into the rooms where the games are going on, I try to do the same, but am stopped at the entrance. Color? Naturally that is the first thought that enters my mind, but nothing is farther away from the minds of the folk in this part of the world. There are certain requirements to be met. My passport. Then several questions are asked me—my hotel, etc. Then I pay ten francs, and start to go in. But there is something else. I did not check my hat and coat, which is compulsory. I understand that no parcels of any kind are permitted inside, and I might have one concealed in my pockets. Said parcel might be a bomb, who knows, so take no chances.

All this being done, I show my ticket and enter. I forgot one other requirement. One must be dressed as a member of the leisure class, and I feel quite flattered at having passed muster on that score. Exquisite politeness! But I know that I am being watched by some of the keenest eyes in Europe, for the Casino has its enemies: the reformers, the cranks, and those who have lost their fortunes. It also has its friends, and I understand it is as difficult to get an article against it published in one of the leading French papers as it is for a Negro to get his side of the story told in a Negro publication supported by White people.

Inside is a striking scene: Magnificent chandeliers, large pictures of women in the nude, tall mirrors, reminding one of the saloons in the dear dead days beyond recall, while around the tables are grouped humanity of all grades, prince and parvenu, vulgar rich, and polite poor, all indiscriminately mixed, intent on trying to guess the correct number as the glistening cylinder of the roulette spins, or as the banker and croupier deal out the cards for trente-quarante (thirty-forty). Some are playing sums that make my head swim, others are playing the minimum, 20 francs, or about 80 cents.

Well, it's my boast that if I were to go even to a cannibal isle, and the feast was ready I'd taste "long-pig" for once, so here goes: I'm going to try my luck. Just 20 francs! But I have no change, only 100 francs, so I hand that to one of the bankers with the intent of buying only one jetton, or chip. But before I can wink my eye he has handed me five, and is off. No alternative but to play them, which I do, one after the other. Well, have you ever seen a famished dog gulp down a tiny scrap of meat? That's the way my 100 francs goes, with swift movements of the little rake.

Well, I've learned one lesson anyway, and that is, the

quickest possible way of getting rid of money.

After that I stand by, fascinated, watching the players. An American with his wife, evidently on their honeymoon. She makes a bet of 5,000 francs ($200) and wins. She doubles and wins again. Lady Luck is with the newlyweds. She has been standing. Now someone rises and she takes a seat. Is she going to repeat the trick of a young American who recently won nearly 1,000,000 francs after starting on a shoestring? Oh, she believes she is. Her face has a flush of victory--$500 this time. The little white ball spins, and the remorseless little rake stretches out and takes her $500 in as carelessly as it took my few pennies. She plays again and again, but Lady Luck has alighted on someone else. She gets up and immediately someone is in her seat.

And so it goes—some winning, some losing, some playing with systems carefully written down in notebooks, others playing by hazards. Two things so far have struck me: One is that the majority of the folk seated at the table are old people, men and women, some of whom move their money onto the numbers with trembling hands. The other thing is how unlike the Colored brother are these folk when they play. But for the low voice of the croupier saying "Faites vos jeux, Messieurs et Dames" (lay your bets, gentlemen and ladies), or "Rien ne va plus" (That's all), all is as quiet as the tomb. And as to excitement, well, it's to be seen only in the hands or the faces of some of the players.

But as to other things, these big White folk are strikingly like some of our Colored folk in Harlem, with their "numbers." They have their charms, dream-books and their superstitions.

For human interest this is the most interesting place I have been in since I left Morocco. I have spent several days around here, and shall tell of some of the above-mentioned things in my next, together with an interview I had with a famous Irish writer, whose recent book about some of the members of the English nobility caused a great stir and gave him no little trouble. He was also once editor and proprietor of a leading publication in America. I asked him what he thought of our race question and shall give his reply.

ROGERS INTERVIEWS FRANK HARRIS IN SOUTHERN FRANCE

Discusses Race Problem With "Greatest Living Writer Of Short Stories"

Former Englishman, Whose Book Is Barred In America, Surprised to Hear Mass of Negroes Aren't Interested in Literature.

Pittsburgh Courier
June 11, 1927
J. A. Rogers

NICE, French Riviera, June 9.—This famous sea-side resort is just a few minutes' ride from Monte Carlo, and is especially noted for its annual carnival.

But before I say anything about it, I must finish my story about the Casino at Monte Carlo.

The regular players and others at the Casino, as I said, are not a whit less superstitious than the Colored "numbers" fans of Harlem. They have their charms: a scarab from an Egyptian tomb; a carved elephant from India; a porte-bonheur from the Congo; a Chinese god, and so on. It is bad luck to look up and catch sight of the pigeons, but if a bird flies through the open window, that's good luck. And the best of all good luck is to have a hunchback near one, or to rub one's hand on his hunch before entering. Some players don't like you to look over their shoulders, you might have the evil eye. And whatever you do never wish that one will win; wish that he will lose.

When the Casino opens in the morning there is a rush to enter that compares favorably with the same on the New York subway. The players want to get their favorite seats, and sometimes hire others to hold them until they come. It is a case of first come, first served, and the politeness, which is so much in evidence here, doesn't work on this occasion.

The favorite table is the one at which the most suicides have occurred, seven in all. Books telling you how surely to win are in abundance. Naturally, too, with all this money floating around, criminals and sharpers from all over the world are attracted here. The latter are exceeded, perhaps, only by the number of detectives male and female.

Now and then a player wins a fortune, but the best proof that the vast majority lose is that the Casino is able to pay out such a huge sum annually to the principality.

A story is told of a man named Jaggers, who won a large fortune by detecting a flaw on one of the cylinders. Not content with playing alone, he hired others to play for him, until the management discovered the cause of his luck. Each morning the tables are tested with a spirit level, as persons have been known to hide themselves in the rooms at night to tamper with the machines. There is also a double lighting system, as bandits once entered the place, descended on the bankers and after robbing them, escaped by putting out the lights. The Sea-Bathing Association, as is the company that runs it is called, has to be wide-awake all the time.

The croupiers get a three months' training before going to a table and it is said that they can let the ball drop in any number they please. This, however, is denied.

If one loses all his money, rather than letting him blow out his brains, the Casino will give him "the viatique," that is, a second-class fare and a little pocket-money to take him back home, which he is supposed to return, or stay out of Monte

Carlo, forever. There is said to be a private graveyard for the suicides; but that may be only a blague, as they say here. It is also said that many individuals that win fortunes are backed secretly by the Casino for advertisement sake. One hears many tales, all of which takes me back to evenings spent with acquaintances of mine in Harlem, whose lives seemed also to center around "the numbers."

Monte Carlo is a heaven or hell; all depends on whether one is winning or not. But in any case, you'll find it one of the most entrancingly beautiful spots on Earth. I can think of nothing more lovely than the harbor of Monaco, its bright blue water, dotted with yachts, while on the hill is the castle in which lives the ruler of the principality, a duchess, whose name has escaped me. [Editor's note: Mr. Rogers is possibly referring to the controversial Charlotte Louise Juliette de Monaco.]

Monaco is also noted for its oceanographic museum. The last ruler, Prince Albert, was very fond of the sea and he traveled around the world seeking specimens. Its aquarium with its remarkable specimens of live octopuses, polyps, and sea-anemones is certainly a sight not to be missed.

In the last article I also told of an interview I had with a famous Irish writer, whose recent autobiography created a very great sensation in England, with considerable repercussion in France and America. This writer is Mr. Frank Harris.

Mr. Harris, who is now 72, was former editor of the London Daily Mail, and counted among his intimate acquaintances such personages as the late King Edward VII, Oscar Wilde, Karl Marx, Sir Henry Irving, Matthew Arnold, Cardinal Newman, Cecil Rhodes, Robert Browning, Ruskin and Lord Randolph Churchill. I should like to repeat a story Mr. Harris tells of the last-named member of the English nobility, but perhaps I had better not. In his book "My Life and Loves" in which he speaks with the utmost possible frankness he lays bare the life, particularly the sex life of some of the great. King Edward, Mr. Harris told me, was particularly fond of hearing naughty stories and on one occasion, the King listened for nearly two hours, while he told him stories. The King, he said, was also at times very sad, and he later discovered that this sadness was due to losses at Monte Carlo. King Edward was a great favorite in this region and there is a statue in his honor facing the harbor of Cannes.

This book is absolutely forbidden in America, and even in France Mr. Harris was hauled into court by his enemies but was discharged. I wish, however, that as many Negroes as possible were able to read that book, as it would certainly help to take the White man off the false pedestal in their minds.

White writers, as late as Jerome Dowd, are forever condemning Negroes for their "unchastity and immorality." These two volumes are a cross section of the White man's life anywhere, and show that Negroes, at least as I know them, are mere novices when it comes to looseness of sexual conduct.

Mr. Harris, when he edited Pearson's, also used to speak out frankly on the race question, and further had as his circulation manager, a Negro, the present editor of Amsterdam News, William M. Kelley. An Irishman, he also used to speak out freely on the Irish question, which got him into the bad graces of the English. In his autobiography he describes a Lord Mayor's banquet with its alleged gluttony, and tells of certain practices of the Lord Mayor, Sir Robert Fowler, during the feast which were so odorous that it made a lady who was sitting beside Sir Robert, flee into the open air. This chapter is a masterpiece in the art of getting back at "the enemy," and is almost as deadly as if he had discharged a gun in their faces. A story like that by a

Negro writer would be more effective than tons of protest.

Mr. Harris was ill, but was kind enough to receive me in his splendid villa, where we talked for more than an hour on Shakespeare on which he is one of the leading authorities, as well as on his travels in Africa, China and other parts. Finally I asked him what he thought of the American race question.

Speaking of the people in America who oppose Negroes because of color, he said:

"It is difficult to believe that human beings can be so savage. Such people keep up a tradition of stupidity that might again cost America very dearly. As for me, I just want the flowers around me so I can see the different species of mankind."

He told of a trip to the South, which he said, he shortened because of the cruelty practiced on the Negro there, and of his disgust at hearing lynching upheld by some of the leading people. "If they were lynching White men for attacking Negro women," he said, "I feel pretty sure there would not be enough rope to go around." The average Southern attitude, he described as "pure hypocrisy" and said that those who shouted most about the alleged superiority of the White race, in his experience, were those who believed it least.

Presently he asked, "Why don't you write a book, exposing these things?" I told him that a book dealing with the race question, as it actually was, stood the slightest possible chance of seeing the light of day, unless the author were prepared to publish it, circulate it, and do everything needed to keep it going himself. Even the White friends of the Negro, while they wanted the truth, wanted just as little of it as possible. I further said that what the publishers wanted were books dealing with the salacious and vicious side of Negro life—a side that has been so thoroughly explored in the last three centuries, that any writer, even partially acquainted with the literature on the Negro, would, if he had anything approaching an original turn of mind, turn for sheer relief to the other side. But this side, I said, the White public did not want to hear as it was contrary to their prejudices.

"But what is the matter with your own publishing firms? Surely they are not afraid to put out books telling the truth?"

I replied that those we had were either interested in religious literature or were aided by White people, who would withdraw their help in that case. "The fact is," I said, "today it is as it was thirty or forty years ago: The people still most interested in Negro literature are White people. The masses of the Negroes, by which I mean about ninety-five per cent don't care whether it goes up or down."

Rising half-way from his couch, he asked emphatically: "Not interested in literature? Then how do they ever hope to get anywhere? The literature of a people is its very life, the memory of the group. Why a people without a literature is almost as badly off as a man without a memory." Mr. Harris, by the way, has been appraised by the American Bookman as "the greatest short story writer living."

Leaving this subject we went on to speak of race prejudice in India. Gandhi and Tagore, he thought perhaps the two greatest human beings alive, and yet, said he, "there are Englishmen who think themselves better than these two men, simply because the latter are Colored men." Color prejudice, he saw, as the rock on which Anglo-Saxon civilization was going to wreck itself. "Why," said he, "a civilization built on a belief is like a set of false teeth. No damned good to anybody."

Later he went on to tell me some of the stories he used to tell King Edward, which kept me laughing for a good half hour—which keep me laughing yet—after which I left feeling that I had met one, who, had been not only in intimate touch with the greatest men of his day, but one to whom sincerity and frankness is almost the breath of his existence. Since then I have been reading his autobiography and a book of short stories he gave me, all of which have helped to make me realize how much farther I, for one, will have to travel in literature.

ROGERS VISITS CLAUDE McKAY IN SOUTHERN FRANCE

Author of "Harlem Shadows" Writing New Book, But Won't Tell Public What It Is About

French Riviera Furnishes New Thrills For Harlem Journalist Still on "Grand Tour"

Pittsburgh Courier
June 18, 1927
J. A. Rogers

CANNES, The French Riviera, June 16. —In this article I will attempt to give a general impression of the French Riviera, together with my visit to Claude McKay, the poet.

Quite a number of towns and villages go to make up the French Riviera—Menton and Cap Martin, Cagnes and Cannes, Beaulieu, Grasse, Cimiez, Nice and many others.

Nice, by far the largest has a population of nearly 200,000, and a history that ante-dates the Christian era by several centuries. It also played an important part in the Christian religion. It was here that the Nicene Creed was written, and here also began the great struggle between the Christian church in Africa and the one in Europe for supremacy. The bone of discussion was whether Christ was equal with God. Later there was another bitter discussion about whether images should be permitted in the churches.

Cimiez, a few minutes ride from Nice, was where the Apostle Barnabas co-worker of Paul, was supposed to have begun his first mission! Here also are the remains of the Roman arena, in which the Christians were thrown to the lions. A popular belief is that the ghosts of the Christians frequent the ruins.

The Moors and Arabs also once conquered or overran all this territory, leaving some of their buildings which are still standing as at Cagnes, and traces of their Negro strain in the faces of the natives. It is possible to have entirely different impressions of Nice, depending on whether one arrives there by land or water. By water one sees fine modern buildings, magnificent hotels, the Casino on its pier extending into the sea, the village of the multi-millionaires dotting the hills at Cimiez, beautiful gardens, and splendid promenades along the waterfront, one of which is named for the United States. From the rear one sees straggling stone houses, built in the Middle Ages, the narrow winding streets of old Italy, and poverty in all its manifestations. In short, the front view is but a beautiful mask for the rear.

In addition to its climate, its gaming resorts, and sports of rare his-others again, much of the Riviera is noted for one other thing; it provides a resort to which those Europeans who are tired of the question of nationality as we are of the one of color, may go for relief.

Several things have contributed toward making the French Riviera about as cosmopolitan a place as is perhaps to be found anywhere else, among which are the following:

Nice was once an independent kingdom with a language of its own, still spoken by the peasants and others; again, much of the Riviera, together with Nice, once belonged to Italy, and was ceded to France in 1860 in payment of a war debt, with the result that while it is not Italian it is not wholly French, just as Canada is not wholly British; further, the proximity of independent Monaco; and lastly the presence of the large numbers of foreigners from all parts of the world, mostly English. Money talks more freely on the Riviera, than anywhere else in Europe. And as to the Negro, tired not only of the color questions, but of the more mischievous one of nationality, this is the ideal spot.

A short ride from Nice, on the other side of Monte Carlo is the town of Menton, perhaps the most beautiful spot on the Riviera, so far as sheer natural beauty is concerned. I stayed there several days and while I have no special love for the hotel-keepers, at least the one with whom I stayed, I must say that the climate is incomparable, even if the prices are also. It is not June but what is so rare as a day at Menton! The broad expanse of ocean; the towering mountains; the picturesque houses dotting the mountain sides; the air like a bracing wine; the orange trees, yellow with fruit; the beautiful gardens; the music playing in the park as it does daily—in short, such a day as will stir others far more prosaic than poets to "fine frenzy."

But all is not a bed of roses on the Riviera. The cost of living is about double what it is in other parts of France. In Menton oranges ripen on tress along the sidewalk but try to buy one and you'll find the price slightly higher than in New York. The poor, here as in other parts of Europe, seem barely able to scrape through life.

Fishing is one of the industries of the poor. Fisher-women, dowdy, gaunt or fat, with black hair flying loose, may be seen helping the men to draw the nets in the morning. They work, a tug-of-war between them and the huge net which they spread out in long lines to dry. And after all that hard work of 20 persons what was the catch that everyone was crowding around to see? Less than a third of a bucket full of silver minnows, so small that one would have difficulty in singling out one.

For three consecutive mornings at Menton the catch was hardly better than that, and on the fourth, the waves were too high for the nets. And after the work with the nets there is the task of beaching the heavy boat. It is no "snap" for the women of the poor here amid all this wealth.

Of course to myself and the other tourists these poor folk are picturesque. They give "color" to the locality and a comfortable feeling of superiority. More and more I am understanding why the good friends of the Negro in the North are so anxious to keep him a Negro, rather than make him a full citizen, and why so many Southern Whites sigh for "the good old darkey days."

Watch closely the faces of many other than the obvious poor and one will find much sadness. This is to be expected of those losing their fortunes at the many Casinos. There is also much broken-down aristocracy from all parts of Europe, chiefly Russia. At the pension at which I stayed was an Italian countess, and that hotel was, well, not exactly one that a countess with something other to count than the number of her ancestors would have selected.

Many of the grand dukes and others who used to live in the front section of Nice have now found themselves in the rear, the moujiks who used to keep them in luxury having decided to put the fruits of their labor to other use. Well, that was Russia. The millionaires from the Southern states still continue to live in their fine villas on the hills of Cimiez.

Next to Monte Carlo, perhaps the most interesting place on the Riviera is the Insectarium at Menton. The excellence of the Riviera climate attracts not only the parasites such as frequent the Casinos, and such as boost the cost of living, but the parasites that live on plants.

These latter parasites, because of the mild climate, find almost no opposition, hence the Insectarium is for the purpose of breeding anti-parasites to save the gardens and orchards, which have been constructed with built-up earth on the sides of the mountains.

Cannes is perhaps the leading yachting center of society, the world over, and yachts from all parts are to be seen in its harbor. Near Cannes is the spot on which Napoleon landed on his return from Elba, as well as the island of St. Marguerite with its castle in which "The Man with the Iron Mask" was imprisoned, and whose identity has always remained a mystery.

Claude McKay

Half-way between Cannes and Nice, and a few minutes ride either way is Antibes, a picturesque town which is more than two thousand years old. There is a great fortress here now used as barracks in which are stationed soldiers, many of whom are Negroes, North Africans, and Cochin Chinese, in the same company with the White soldiers. There is no color line in the French army.

Arriving here, I hurried to look up McKay and found him living in the oldest part of the town, and contrary to my expectation, looking healthy, and weighing more than when I had seen him last in America. For several years he had been ill most of the time. He was hard at work on a book, but what it was he would not tell. I spent several days in the town, and although we talked on almost every other subject, he was reticent about his work, though it seems that most of his poems now go to White magazines. [Editor's Note: It is likely that this book is either the best selling novel "Home to Harlem," "Banjo" (both published in 1929) or "Banana Bottom" published in 1933.]

McKay, it will be recalled, is the author of "Harlem Shadows," and came into considerable publicity, when a group of leading Negroes visited Congress during the series of race riots that occurred after the war, and after reading his poem "If We Must Die," to the congressmen, told them that that was the spirit of the newer generation of Negroes, who had decided to suffer massacre with impunity no longer. The poem together with the address of the delegation were published in the Congressional Record. As to the date and the names of the delegations, I have forgotten them. [Editor's note: McKay is writing about the riots in Harlem and throughout the U.S. in 1919. Senator Henry Cabot Lodge, Sr., read this poem into the Congressional record during World War II after this delegation, mentioned by Rogers, addressed the Congress.]

"If We Must Die," is really the Marseillaise of the American Negro, and that so many of us are unacquainted with it is because we do not have the spirit of those French peasants of 1793, who decided they were men, and not beasts of burden for the nobility. I once heard one of our leading White critics, who passes for Colored, tell an audience that that poem and others of similar nature in the book were not poetry, the influence being that they did not tell of skylarks and sunsets, violets, stars, and the like, but dealt with fierce human passions after the manner of Deborah's song after her triumph over Sisera, The Watch on the Rhine, or the Marseillaise. The critic in question has himself experienced a minimum of color prejudice, if any.

"Harlem Shadows," covers a wide range—from lynching to the wind in the New York subway. It was abundantly praised by critics of both groups, and that thousands of the book still remain on the shelves of the publishers, while the author is in want is, in truthful, if not polite English, certainly no credit to us.

The publishers of "Harlem Shadows" are Harcourt, Brace & Co., New York. It sells for two dollars.

ROGERS TOLD IN PARIS INTERVIEW WHY LIBERIA OUSTED GARVEYITES

Colonel Davis, Aid to President King, Says Wealthy American Negroes Welcome in Africa

Courier Correspondent Sees President King Honor French Unknown Soldier; Says Liberia Is Credit to Race

Pittsburgh Courier
June 25, 1927
J. A. Rogers

PARIS, June 23.—In spite of a heavy rain, a large crowd of Parisians flocked to the Arc de Triomphe de l'Etoile here to witness the ceremony of the laying of a wreath on the tomb of the Unknown Soldier by President C. D. B. King of Liberia, now on a European tour.

Accompanying the president were his aide-de-camp Col. T. Elwood Davis of the Liberian army; Capt. Charles T. King, son of the president, and secretary to Col. Davis; Mrs. C. A. King, Miss Ellen King, Master C. B. D. King, Jr., and Mrs. M. D. Ketter of Liberia. In addition there were the attaches of the Liberian Legation, Baron Rudolph Leman, and Baron Bogarde, and the Baronnesse Bogarde, as well as several leading French officials.

The president, dark, tall, a striking figure in a black coat, with Col. Davis on his right in a well-fitted military uniform descended from his automobile at the hour set for the ceremony and walked up to the tomb between the ranks of the bright-Colored French Republican Guard. Here after a short silent prayer, he laid the wreath, a magnificent one of roses and hyacinths, with the colors of the Liberian Republic, on the tomb under the great arch, while the crowd stood by reverently with doffed hats. The ceremony, though simple, was a very touching one—this head of the single republic in Africa paying his tribute to the valor of the leading republic on a neighboring continent.

At the conclusion of the ceremony, the crowd which had been kept back by the gendarmes flocked to the president's carriage to get a closer glimpse of him, while photographers leveled their cameras at the party.

The Liberian ladies were becomingly dressed in spite of the rain, in styles, which if not Parisian, in cut showed that the ladies of the far republic are not a whit behind the French capital in matters of elegance. All in all the ensemble and bearing of the Liberian party was one that generally reflected credit on the Negro race, everywhere.

President King, as was said, is here with his party on an European tour, arriving recently in Paris from Bordeaux, where a special car was provided for him by the French government. Leaving Monrovia, the French steamship line, Chargeurs Reunis, placed the entire first class deck at his disposition.

Arriving at the St. Laxare station, Paris, President King and party were met by Col. Phillippe, aide-de-camp to President Doumergue, Deputy Blaise Diagne of Senegal, Col. Becq de Fouquieres, and other French officials. Several functions have been given here in honor of President King.

Later the Paris representative of the Pittsburgh Courier called on President King for an interview chiefly relative to the migration of American Negroes to Liberia. The president, who was engaged in a conference directed his aide, Col. Davis to speak for him.

As to the matter of immigration, Col. Davis, who is a native of Indiana, said that American Negroes were very welcome in Liberia, and that business opportunities were unusually good. Nevertheless, he pointed out that any immigration to Liberia would at this time have to be a selective one, just as in the case of White colonies to Canada and Australia. "Liberia," said Col. Davis, "is not in a position to care for dependents. What it needs in the matter of immigration are persons with capital, and most of all skilled farmers. There are splendid opportunities for persons with from five to six thousand dollars. Right now there is a fine opening for a haberdashery and a tailoring and cleaning establishment."

Another requisite, said Col. Davis, is that immigrants should be of a type sympathetic to the republic, as persons of the radical discontented type were likely to embroil the government with neighboring European powers, some of whom are anxious for any pretext to seize Liberian soil. "That was one of the reasons," he said, why the Liberian government had to oust the Garvey Movement, and prevent the landing of Garvey's officials on Liberian soil.

"The Universal Negro Improvement Association had landed shipping supplies, building materials and even a temporary residence all ready to be set up for Garvey himself, 375 miles down the coast at a spot where such a proceeding was likely to get us into trouble with one of the big European powers, all of whom watch this sort of thing carefully on their African soil."

"Let us suppose that at this spot in question any trouble had arisen during which a subject of another country was hurt, why, it would have been easy for that country to claim indemnity, or to invade us saying that we are not able to maintain order."

"American Negroes are most welcome—the proof is that I am one myself, being a naturalized Liberian. The type we do not want however, is that of a man, named John Hall, who recently migrated to Liberia from Pennsylvania. Hall, whom we had permitted to land with his goods, in which were several thousand rounds of ammunition, was responsible for a tragedy unknown to the history of the republic. Some weeks ago some soldiers were returning from parade, when one of them accidentally fell against his booth, knocking it over. In the altercation that followed, Hall shot the man dead, then a lieutenant and a policeman, and fled to the home of his lawyer, where he barricaded himself, heavily armed. From this place he killed several others, and finally the place had to be burned down with the murderer in it."

"Doctors, dentists, business men, electrical engineers, farmers, we are glad to get. In fact, Liberia prefers American Negroes and American goods."

Speaking of the rubber industry, Col. Davis said that that was getting along well, but that Liberia was very far from deserting its most famous product, Liberian coffee. Plassava, a fibre that grows wild in the swamps, he said, was finding a splendid market in Europe, as well as palm products.

The presence of an independent Negro government in Africa means much to the future of the Negro race the world over, said Col. Davis. Africa with her vast almost untouched resources is the coming continent. Col. Davis admitted that Garvey had done a wonderful work in advertising Africa to the Negro peoples, and that he had some splendid ideas but that Garvey himself was not the right one to put them into execution.

The reporter left with the impression that this little Black republic with its great natural resources was through no fault of its own in a somewhat ticklish international position, and hence had to watch the type of immigrant it admitted. At present American Negroes are barred from most parts of Africa.

After visiting Holland, Belgium, Germany, Switzerland, Italy, and possibly England, President King will return to Liberia, arriving there in time for his inauguration in January, 1928. He was recently reelected by a great majority.

[Editor's note: In 1986 this election was recorded into the Guinness Book of World Records as "the most fraudulent election in history." This is because King is reported to have received 234,000 votes, with only 15,000 registered voters.]

ROGERS MEETS "HOMESICK" AMERICAN NEGROES IN MARSEILLES, FRANCE

Says France Is Fine While Money Lasts; No Color Line In Best Hotels, He Finds

Visits Town With Large Negro Population and Finds Race Relations Amicable

Pittsburgh Courier
July 2, 1927
J. A. Rogers

MARSEILLES, FRANCE, June 30.—It is not until one has traveled around Southern Europe a bit, seeing old and still older cities, that he begins to realize what a very new country America is after all. The nearest comparison I can think of is one of those venerable giants of the California forests and a very young oak.

This city of nearly a million souls is more than 2,500 years old, that is about eight times the age of New York City, and more than 2,000 years older than the oldest city in the New World. Known under the Romans as Massillia, it was the great rival sea port of Carthage. Readers of Roman history will recall that it was once destroyed by Julius Caesar in his quarrel with Pompey.

Here, it is also that Mary Magdalene and Lazarus, the one that was said to have been raised from the dead by Christ, came as the first missionaries. Napoleon won considerable fame here, too, when as a young man he used his artillery against the Royalists. This city, it is, too, from which the name of the French national anthem was derived. Marseilles, then, a hot-bed of revolt was the first to adopt the stirring song of Rouget de L'Isle.

Since humanity has been living on this same spot for so many generations, the appearance of the city, or more correctly the part of it, that is known as Le Vieux Port (The Old Port), has a very antiquated appearance. Narrow, winding streets, on which the sun rarely shines; buildings so aged in places that a regular network of props for them fill certain of the streets; filthy, dissolute looking lanes with clothing and bed linen in all stages of deterioration, strung across; odorous humanity, swarming over the rough cobblestones, piling in and out of the shops, or driving sharp bargains at the stalls which so fill the streets that the crowd must filter through almost in Indian file. The impression, all in all, is that of visiting the house of a poor and very old man, with its plaster falling loose; its window panes filled with aged newspapers, and all the cheap old furniture and utensils of several generations ago.

The city, of course, has its aristocratic sections. Nearby is one of the most famous thoroughfares in Europe; "The Cannebiere," with its splendid shops, fine hotels, and its railroad station with a marble stairway the equal of any I have seen.

Marseilles will be of particular interest to Negroes, because of its large Colored population, which in actual numbers is second to only two others in Europe, Constantinople and Paris. And so far as percentage is concerned I believe it is much higher than Paris.

There are two Negro regiments, as well as other Negroes, who are in the White regiments—Marseilles, is the headquarters of a French Army corps. In addition there are Negroes from Africa, the French and British West Indies, the United States, Madagascar and elsewhere. Perhaps the most of them originally came as sailors, and they are so numerous that one almost fancies himself back in a Negro neighborhood in America. The great majority are what are known as full-blooded

Negroes, a person of a lighter skin being rare.

Nearly all live in the Old Port, and with all these Negroes living among these poor Whites, I was interested to know how, what we in America call race relations, were. I began to question almost every Negro I met until I had talked with perhaps not less than a hundred, sometimes with not less than fifteen at a time. The British West Indian and the American Negroes seemed especially glad to see me, and quickly brought others to meet me when they heard that I was a writer for the newspapers.

The majority these latter were about the most homesick lot of human beings I have ever met. They had come to Marseilles, which is the leading seaport of the Mediterranean, or had drifted there in the hopes of finding a ship to take them home. One young man from Virginia was in a state of rags equal to that of a Casablanca Arab. "Would you like to get back to America?" I asked him. "Would I?" he replied, "If I could swim it I'd start back tomorrow." Of course, one of the reasons I found them all so eager to talk with me was that they were all expecting to make a "touch," and usually finished by asking me to help them. I have never wished so hard before that I was wealthy.

Questioning about the attitude of the White people I found, after a time, that I was getting two different sets of replies. One was to the effect that Negroes found it difficult to get along, the reason being the French men did not like their association with the White women, and would not give them work. One of the men who told me this is married to a rather distinguished looking blonde. The other reply was to the effect that there was no color prejudice of any sort, that the French people treated them sometimes even better than their own poor people, and that as to their association with the White women nobody seemed to notice it. For instance, both the British West Indians and the Americans told me that they reported at the docks daily, that sometimes the employers taking them for Colored Frenchmen gave them work, which sometimes they were unable to hold because they did not understand the language. Both West Indians and Americans told me that they found France a paradise "while the money lasted, " but that with it gone it was about as near to the other place as they ever wanted to get. "Too much misery here," said one of them. And indeed I saw some of the White people so far down that they seemed hardly human. Quite as bad as those I saw in Morocco or Naples.

As to the French West Indians, when I asked them whether there was any color prejudice everyone answered in the negative. Some of them were officers and non-commissioned officers in the White regiment and they told me that they received the same treatment as the White men. As I said before there is no color line in the French army. Negroes, Caucasians, Indo-Chinese and others being indiscriminately mixed in some regiments and military schools.

Next I talked with several White persons, policemen, bartenders, beggars and others, and everyone said there had never been any kind of racial disturbances. In the bar rooms I saw Negroes sitting at the same table with White men and women, while in one or two with some sort of a jazz band I saw only very dark men with White women, the proprietor in each case being White.

In the dance halls in which lively music was kept going all the time, I saw pretty much the same thing. And the dives, some of which I visited! The Black sailors who had landed that day with their money still burning a hole in their pockets were receiving as much attention from the ladies—I shall not attempt to describe some of these dives except to say that if St. Peter has any sense of humor he is going to prepare just such a purgatory for Negro-hating crackers. Of course, I have seen the same thing in California and Utah with their law against race mixing, as well as in Chicago, with the difference, of course, that there it was under cover.

The same conditions exist in England and in Europe generally where because of the absence of Colored women the only female company is White, just as in parts of Africa, with its absence of White women, the only female company for the White men, is Black. To be frank, neither of the two males in question seem to pine very much about the absence of their own women.

As I said I met many Negroes who said that they found difficulty in getting work because of the alleged jealousy of the Frenchmen. In view of what I saw I was inclined to discount what they said until a lady gave me the key: "Oh," she said, "those are Sidis." That is to say they are North Africans, which are not popular for several reasons, the first and foremost of which is not a difference of color but of culture.

The North Africans are alleged to be none too clean; they are accused of being as fond of cutting up people with knives as a Mississippi White is addicted to the use of the rope or the torch to settling his grievances. One reads not infrequent reports of these butcheries in the French papers. Among other reasons is the fact that the North African is usually a Mohammedan, while the other Negroes are Christian.

At the time of writing this there was a shortage of work in Marseilles and we have always heard it said that when Black and White meet and there is a shortage of work, with Black men getting work while some White men have nothing to do there will be racial disturbance. I, myself, have said it over and over and have attributed the Chicago riot mainly to this cause. But there is an analogous situation in France, a White man's land, and yet White and Black live in harmony. There are no racial commissions, no collectors of data, no reconciliation movements, no inter-racial societies. In short if one does not bring up the race question himself, he is hardly likely to encounter it.

Again, in many towns in America as say Salt Lake City, Los Angeles, Ogden, as well as places in the Canadian Northwest all analogous to Marseilles so far as Colored population is concerned, Negroes are rarely permitted in White places. In Los Angeles I was refused service in many places, while here I ate in one of the best restaurants. I met a New York globe trotter and musician, named Earl Granstaff, a dark Negro, of whom I shall have more to say later, living in one of the best hotels on the Cannebiere. Why is it when Negroes migrate to Chicago or Carteret, there is a riot, and why when they migrate to a French town, like Marseilles, there is none, for the Colored population of Marseilles is quite recent. A Colored American in the consular service tells me that before the war, he and another Colored man were the only two Negroes there and that they were regarded as curiosities.

What I believe this phenomenon to be I shall give in my next chapter, together with the account of my trip to the Chateau made famous by Alexander Dumas and his Monte' Cristo.

ROGERS FINDS INTERESTING RACE HISTORY IN FRANCE

Writer Finds Race Grossly Misrepresented By American Motion Pictures In Europe

Says Every Other People Except Negro Has Bureau In Europe to Offset Vicious Propaganda

Pittsburgh Courier
July 9th, 1927
J. A. Rogers

AVIGNON, FRANCE, June 30.—This city on the River Rhine is in Provence—a region of great historical interest. Long before Christ the Phoenicians, a people of Ethiopian decent sailed up the river, and established a colony here. After them came the Greeks, and still later the Romans. This region, as students of Latin will recall, was known as Gallia Narbonensis. After the Romans came the Teutons, who were finally defeated in one of the greatest battles of all times by Caius Marius (See Plutarch's "Lives of Illustrious Men.")

Still later came Hannibal, the famous African general, who accomplished the stupendous feat of crossing the Alps with his army. From Tarascon, a nearby town, one gets a fine view of the mountains crossed by Hannibal and later by Napoleon.

Following them came the Visigoths and the Vandals, the same that descended on Rome, with the determination to wipe out all trace of her. After them came the Moroccans, who after their victory over the Spaniards crossed the Pyrenees and held most of this part of France until defeated by Charles Marte at the Battle of Tours in 732 A.D. Mohammedanism, up to that time had been victorious over Christianity, and but for the defeat of Abdul Rahman, the Moorish leader as well as for disaffection in the Mohammedan empire in Africa, all Europe might have been Moslem. Thereafter the power of these Negroid peoples began to wane until they were driven back into Africa. Tours was one of the decisive battles of the world, and its loss set back the progress of the Negro race at least a thousand years.

After the Moors came the Normans from England under Richard of the Lion Heart, on their way to the Holy Land to wrest, as they said the tomb of the Saviour from the "infidel Turk," but really to despoil the then declining Mohammedan empire.

And so with all these invasions it may be imagined that the Provencals are a very much mixed people. One could have gone further back than the Phoenicians for there are relics of the Stone Age on the River Var, and the Europeans of those days as some of the leading anthropologists, like Sergi and Ripley, say were descended from the same stock as the Negroes. Hence when our American scientists speak of a pure White race one has to listen with a smile of indulgence, for what is true of Provence is true of all Europe.

Naturally, too, historic monuments of all these civilizations are to be found. At Aries, a nearby town are the ruins of a Greek temple, which was said to have been destroyed by Deacon Cyril, an over-zealous Christian. In this town there is also an old Roman arena, where the Christians used to be thrown to the lions. Today a form of bull fight is held in the arena. The practice is to snatch off the ribbons tied to the neck of the bull.

At Nimes, nearby, is another miniature Coliseum, seating 80,000. This arena, also, is in good preservation, and regular bull fights are held at certain periods, during which the best bull fighters are brought from Spain. There are also the remains of the Temple of Diana.

At San Remy, near by, is a triumphal arch built by Julius Caesar and as fine as any in Rome. At Avignon are Roman aqueducts not much inferior to those of Rome. It is in this region that has been discovered some of the most famous old statues, as that of the Venus Genetrix.

But undoubtedly the most remarkable thing in all Provence is the Palace of the Popes, which is, in reality an immense fortress, and certainly the most formidable structures of its kind I have ever seen. Its sides look like giant cliffs. And the circumference of the ramparts I have been told is three miles.

The Popes moved up here from Rome between 1809 and 1879, a period that is known as "the Babylonian Captivity of the Popes." If it is so called, as I suppose it is, because the period was the same length as that spent by the Jews in Babylon then there is certainly a fine irony behind it, for while the Jews were so unhappy that they refused to sing "the Lord's song in a strange land," the Popes lived here in a splendor that rivaled the Caesars. Or is it because the practices of some of these Popes were Babylonish? It was indeed a long way from St. Peter in the Catacombs to his spiritual descendants in this grim but sumptuous palace.

The most noteworthy objects in this palace are the tombs of the Popes Innocent VI, and John XXII, and the Hall of Justice.

At Villeneuve-les-Avignon, not far away, are the ruins of the summer palace of the Popes—Chateaueuf-du-Pape—also the name of the famous wine, once used exclusively for cooling the palates of thirsty prelates. Avignon, as in the days of the Popes, is the center of a great wine district, and it seems as difficult here to avoid drinking wine as to escape hootch at home, which is saying a great deal.

France, it is said, lost a great deal of revenue when America decided to change to her brand of liquor. Well, if France still has a deficit on this score, it is certainly not the fault of the American tourists.

Avignon was also noted for its harsh laws against the Jews, one of which decreed that "Jews and prostitutes shall not touch fruit exposed for sale," and if they did they would be compelled to buy what they have touched. Another was that if they cohabited with a Christian woman, or entered "or dared to think of entering the red light district," the penalty would be "the loss of a leg and 25 pounds sterling for each offense." Among other things, such as being compelled to wear a separate garb they weren't allowed to shave Christians, including perhaps the ladies, many of whom wore bobbed hair in those days. The Christians of those days weren't so far behind the Southern Whites in sex jealously, after all. (See "Laws of Avignon" by Louis de Pileur, and the Jewish Encyclopedia).

It is not until one gets in this region that he begins to meet the real French people for Marseilles and the Riviera, like Paris, are more cosmopolitan than French. The folks are very polite here, more, I might say that with my rougher American manners I find them disconcertingly polite. Almost everything that can be done is done to avoid giving the least offense. As to the peasantry they seem quite contented with their surroundings and quite as blissfully indifferent about what is going on elsewhere as the average Negro.

Many of the peasants speak a French of their own—the Provencal—and I had as much difficulty understanding it as I had the mixture of French and Italian at Menton or the peasants in Yorkshire and Cornwall, England. Provencal seems to be a mixture of French and Spanish. Colored folk are as scarce in this region as silver money in France. I saw only one, a native of Martinique, by the singular name of Germany. Monsieur J. Germany, who won most of the medals given by the French in the last war, is an inspector of customs. I met him on the train at Tarascon, and a delightful old lady who was in the compartment went on over him as if he were a long lost son. Monsieur Germany is a very dark man, but that makes no difference here. His name, by the way, will sound singular only to English ears, for the word for "German" in French "Allegmagne."

But I have discovered these days it is absolutely impossible to escape the color question. I went to a moving picture theater and there was an American picture with Negroes in it doing the usual niggerisms, just as in Milan there was the odious "Birth of a Nation." Is it any wonder that the majority of Europeans who think about the American Negro at all think he must be either a jazz player or a servant after seeking the movies, most of which are American.

Contrast this with a French film I saw, "Yasmina." One of the stars is Benglia, a very dark Negro woman I mentioned two years ago as playing at the Folies-Bergere in Paris. Benglia and the Japanese, Sessue Hayakawa are two screen actors that will always be green in my memory. Both say little but by some mysterious force they are able to convey by a look, by a single gesture that which calls for no end of motion on the part of the average movie actors. The Negro, in this film, was not shown as a grinning servant as in the other film, but rather as one who was capable of the highest feeling, the noblest sentiment. Again, the officer in command of the firing squad that was to shoot the hero was a Negro, while most of the men under him were White.

And as to the picture itself were it to be shown in the States, folks would break down the door to get in. There is a harem scene in it in which the women step into the water clad only in their skins.

The American Negro is much misrepresented throughout Europe by these pictures, and while every other oppressed group has an agency or mission in London, Rome, Paris, Berlin and the other capitals to offset propaganda against them, the American Negro sometimes stronger both in wealth and actual numbers is doing nothing.

At Tarascon is the Church of St. Martha, in which Martha, the sister of Mary and Lazarus, was said to have been buried. If I remember rightly the tomb is said to have been rifled by the Arabs, and the sacred relics thrown out. However, at the present time, a skull said to be hers is still shown, and may be seen for three francs.

At another town further south are the relics of Mary, whose body was said to have been discovered several hundred years later after her death in such perfect preservation that a delicious odor came from the coffin, while at the same time fennel grew from her tongue. The spot where Christ touched her on her forehead had retained the same color as if she were alive. (I am telling all this with the same straight face with which I heard it.)

In connection with the Church of St. Martha is the tradition of St. Sarah, an Ethiopian woman, who fled from Palestine with Mary, Martha, and Lazarus. St. Sarah is held in great veneration by the gypsies.

Tarascon is also the scene of one of the most delightful stories ever written "Tartarin of Tarascon," in which Alphonse Daudet indulges in gentle satire at the expense of the Provencals.

This section of Provence is also noted for its silk worms,

or magnans, as they are called. Not far away is the city of Lyons, whose chief industry is silk manufacture and where I spent a day on my way to Geneva. My next article will be on Geneva and the League of Nations.

IS THE STAR OF THE FOLIES-BERGERE REALLY MARRIED?

Rogers Discloses Amazing "Truths" of Josephine Baker's Reported Marriage to Count

Repeated Denials and Affirmations Put Dancer In Embarrassing Position—Search of Records Does Not Reveal License—Popularity Said to Be Waning

Pittsburgh Courier
July 16, 1927
J. A. Rogers

PARIS, FRANCE, July 14.—Is Josephine Baker, star of the Folies-Bergere, really married, or is the story of her reported marriage only an advertising stunt? Is the Count de Savatini, or Abatino, only a cabaret dancer and a no-Count, that was to play the part of a Count in a movie picture, or is he, as Miss Baker claims, the descendant of a noble Sicilian family?

A few days ago three English speaking papers, the Paris edition of the Chicago Tribune; the New York Herald, and the continental edition of the London Daily Mail, carried stories to the effect that Miss Baker was married to the "Count." Later, that day, accompanied by Charles H. Johnson of Atlanta, Ga., here on a visit, I called on Miss Baker at the Folies-Bergere, when in answer to a letter I had written her that morning, she said: "Yes, we're married." Previously both Dr. Johnson and myself had been talking to the "Count," who was waiting for Miss Baker in a taxi, and he said that he had been married to Miss Baker. Among the things he wanted to know was whether the papers I represented were in Paris. This question he asked me several times, each time I told him that they were in America. Our introduction to the "Count" was made by Spencer Williams. Miss Baker also told me that the stories in the White papers were true, her only objection being the manner in which they showed her speaking.

Later Spencer Williams, well known song writer, told us that he was a witness at the wedding and on Dr. Johnson's inquiry told us several other things highly complimentary about Miss Baker. Two of these were that Miss Baker had saved more than seven million francs—the Count and herself being very careful managers—and that Miss Baker had bought a villa in Monte Carlo. The only people who would be found speaking against Miss Baker, said Williams, are the Colored people in Paris. We left with the firm conviction that Miss Baker was married to the "Count."

One fact struck me at the time, none of the French papers carried anything about the marriage, except in the advertisement carried in them by the Folies-Bergere. This read in English:

"The truth! The Black star, Josephine Baker, has made only a White marriage—and she will continue to appear in 'A Burst of Folly' at the Folies-Bergere."

Three days later, however, one of the leading French papers carried on its front page (Issue of June 24), the following story of which this is a correct translation:

-It was a trick! Josephine Baker is a Countess only in name-

Has Josephine Baker really become Countess d'Albertini, as the newspapers say?

That is what we have asked the dancer, who received us with a great burst of laughter, followed it is true with a little confusion.

"Yes, I am a Countess," she told us at first. Then with a little pirouette she added:

"At least in the movies—a movie I play that Maurice Dekobra has written and still without a title, and in which my very nice manager, Pepito Abatino, and I are going to play."

"Listen, do you know a gentleman with a brown mustache, who resembles Adolphe Menjou? It is he, my husband in the films, isn't it?"

"Then how amusing it was to be married. I have even let the city believe that story a little. Ah, how false news spreads! What I told several friends as a joke all the world has taken as serious."

She pouted as a frolicsome child who fears to be chided. "Will the public be angry, you think? It has been so nice."

Her voice became almost suppliant. "How funny it is to be called 'Mrs.' to receive telegrams from all parts of the world. Don't all young girls desire to be called 'Mrs.' some time?"

"They are already talking of getting me a divorce." A burst of laughter. "Don't you think it would be difficult to get a divorce with the film still unfinished, since I am 'Mrs.' only in the film." And she concluded laughing.

"What is perhaps true, that is the best way of getting married after all."

On reading this article I at once called at the American Embassy, where the "Count and Countess" were said to have been married by Ambassador Herrick. "Ridiculous!" I was informed there, "even the son of the ambassador couldn't be married here."

Next I went to the American Consulate, where I met George W. Mitchell, native of North Carolina, who has been a receiver in the consular service for twenty-one years. "They were not married here," he said, "and what's more four French detectives have come here to find out if the story is true. Miss Baker gets a big salary, I understand, and a change of name would make a difference in her income tax. The detectives tell me that they have searched every mayor's office in the city, and there is no record of any marriage. Besides if Miss Baker was married don't you think it would be at the Italian Consulate?"

My next visit was to the office of the Daily Mail to hear how they had got the story as well as the picture of the dancer and the alleged Count. "I am glad I didn't touch that story," said the editor, "it was just an advertising trick." I am glad that we said under the picture that we got the story from the Tribune."

At the Tribune I saw the editor, Mr. Ranger. "We have lost all confidence in Miss Baker," he said, "we heard of the story and sent a reporter down there. He asked Miss Baker if she were really married, and she said, 'Yes, don't you think it is a wonderful thing.' And so we carried the story believing it to be true."

At the office of the Herald I heard a similar story. "There was a big bunch of reporters down at Miss Baker's cabaret," said the editor. It will be noted however, that not a single French paper carried the story of the alleged marriage.

Shortly before I had called on Miss Baker and she had told me that she was engaged to an Italian Count, who is an artist. She also said that she had been offered $1,500 a night in some place, in Vienna. I think, though people would hardly believe that to be true. The fact is that she has told every reporter, including myself that she had married a Count, a story that now seems to be highly improbable, and only an advertising stunt that the management of the Folies quickly capitalized.

The truth is that Miss Baker has been steadily losing vogue in Paris. When I visited the Folies I was much disappointed to find that it was not her, but an English dancer, Jack Sanford, who was the hit of the show. Her dancing was not as good as that of many girls I have seen at the Lincoln or the Lafayette in New York, though I heard that her dancing last year was very good.

When I arrived in Paris a Lady who knows Miss Baker well says that the account carried about her last year in New York World, and reproduced in all the Colored papers was grossly exaggerated. The general impression is that the present incident is going to do her a great deal of harm. The English speaking editors, are of course, all angry over the incident, and to indulge in a little free language, you can't kill them for that.

Finally, just before mailing this I called at the Folies-Bergere, and saw Spencer Williams who admitted that the Paris-Soir was right. "The story of the marriage was just an advertising ruse," he said, "though when Miss Baker announced it that night I really thought it was true."

In the meantime "the Count," who is only a minor employee in a department of the Italian government is much worried over the affair for reasons which shall be nameless. As was said, he asked me several times which paper I represented.

"Countess" Josephine and "Flo" Mills Rival White Actors, Claim

In view of the almost phenomenal rise of the charming American actress, Josephine Baker, from an insignificant "extra girl" to the "Darling of Paris" and to the toast of the Montmarte, and the rapid ascent to fame of the clever, alluring Florence Mills to the talk of London, a White "special" writer has commented on these two stories of accomplishment. The great success of these two girls has been the talk of theatrical circles for the past few months. Miss Baker's glowing career was particularly noticed when it was reported that she had married a Roman Count.

Realizing the significance of the great achievement of these two Colored girls in foreign lands, Milton Bronner, Special Writer for The Press, contributes the following article from London:

"Actresses and musicians and dancers and cabaret girls and novelists and poets have come here from America and often they have been favorably received by the general public of London and Paris. But if the truth must be told the triumphs of John Barrymore, Jane Cowl, Doris Keane, Paul Whiteman and all the rest pale into insignificance before the knockout of two Colored girls—Florence Mills and Josephine Baker.

The lithe Josephine came to Paris almost unheralded. She first appeared at the swell Champs Elysees theater in a show called simply "'Revue Negre'—Negro Review. It was a singing and dancing show, such as we have been familiar with for donkey's years. But soon all the Parisian cognoscenti were flocking to the house. And then suddenly the show disappeared from the swell Etoile district. The reason was not failure. It was success.

The Folies-Bergere claimed Josephine at a huge salary. She's been packing the house ever since. Her form has been done by French sculptors. Her face has been painted by French artists. She has opened a cabaret of her own. Her vogue goes on undiminished.

Something of the same sort happened with Florence Mills. She, too, came unheralded. London was simply informed that she was to appear in a Negro review called 'Blackbirds.' It caught on at once, largely due to Florence. The show is now in its third edition and promises to run on all through the summer and on and on indefinitely. The Prince of Wales has been to see the performance over and over again. Society has followed in his wake.

But I have kept the best for the last. Nowadays if a woman wants a certain shade of creamy brown silk stockings, she doesn't describe it as such. Not at all. If she is shopping in London she simply says: 'I want that new
Florence Mills shade.'

Or if she is in Paris, she says to the salesgirl:

'Let me see that new Josephine Baker shade.'

Now that's real fame. Nellie Melba, world renowned opera singer, once had an ice named after herself, peche Melba. But I never heard of an English cigarette being named after Barrymore, nor a perfume after June Cowl, nor a face powder after Doris Keane."

ROGERS, ILL IN PARIS HOSPITAL, SPEAKS UP FOR PULLMAN PORTERS

Says It Is Time Race Workers Quit Enriching Others; Urges Porters to Support Brotherhood
Charges Pullman Company Has Made Millions Off Porters' Tact With Public, But Has Miserly Underpaid Them

Pittsburgh Courier
September 3, 1927
J. A. Rogers

{The Pittsburgh Courier's Editor's Note: Mr. J. A. Rogers, who, from 1909 to 1919 was a Pullman Porter, and whose series of four articles on Paris has been broken by an attack of typhoid fever from which he is now suffering in the American Hospital of Paris, wrote this article in defense of the Pullman Porters, by special request of the The Courier, when cruising in the Mediterranean from Gibraltar to Sicily. The Courier has three other articles from Mr. Rogers written from Italy which will be published during his inability to write, because of illness.

Next week Mr. Roy Lancaster, Secretary-Treasurer of the Brotherhood of Porters, will give a complete survey of the movement from its inception to the present, and will incidentally answer some pertinent questions that knockers have been asking Brotherhood men.}

PARIS, France, September 1.—Today, as in the days of slavery, the chief beneficiaries of color prejudice, and the various devices used for keeping the Negro "in his place" are the employers of labor.

Among the foremost of these beneficiaries is the Pullman Company, which in the past half century has profited to the tune of several hundred millions of dollars. And not only insofar as actual labor is concerned, but in the quality of the service rendered, for prior to the war the Pullman Company, and to some extent the dining car service, were the only places open, generally speaking, to the intelligent Negro with aspirations to an income above that of an ordinary porter or ditch-digger. The war has helped to open better employments to no small extent.

In the Pullman Company—I am speaking chiefly of the years 1909 to 1919, with which I am best acquainted—could be found men with the inherent ability to fill any position in the company from the presidency downwards, but because of color these were all thrust into the humble, but none the less very essential position (to the company) of porter. Among these were graduates of some of the leading universities, doctors, lawyers, ministers, holders of scientific degrees and others above the level of intelligence of White men in similar occupations. It is safe to say that no other kind of unskilled labor in America could and can show as high a grade of intellectual development as that of the Pullman Porter. The kind of porter described in "From 'Superman' to Man," (one of my books) I can assure readers, was not rare, nor is the story autobiographical. Time and again, I met men, who simply dazzled me with their learning, or with their ability to draw, play music or speak languages. Repeatedly, has a porter, graduate of some leading medical college, given first aid to the injured at a wreck, or to a sick passenger. Many of these men, it is true, were merely earning enough to make a start in chosen occupation, but a large portion were staying permanently, mainly because there was no opening for them in the White business world, or because they lacked the spirit of daring and preferred the certain pay of $25 a month and tips, rather than venture out on their own initiative.

In the White world intellectual development and occupation usually go hand in hand. To find it otherwise is rare. An intelligent White man who enters almost any field will pretty soon find himself promoted, almost in spite of himself. To say that this is not true of a Negro, is to utter a fact so well-known that the mere calling attention to it, incites boredom. For instance, the case of the Pullman conductor. I met hundreds of conductors and while some of them were intelligent and temporarily out of a better job, the vast majority would have been street car conductors, elevator starters, grocery clerks and the like, out of the Pullman service. The duties of a Pullman conductor demands no higher training than that of an eighth grade school boy, and can easily be done by the average porter, many of whom, running on a train that carries a single sleeper, are in charge. Such porters do on that sleeper, all that is expected of the White conductor. The only qualification demanded of such a porter is a minimum of two years service, and a willingness to accept a little less than half the pay of the White conductor, who, in short, occupies the superior position, almost solely by virtue of complexion.

No matter in what walk of life you are, intelligence, trained or untrained, is a tremendous asset—an asset that outweighs all other factors—hence, the depreciation of intelligence, when its covering is a dark skin, has contributed enormously to the quality of service the Pullman service has been able to give the public, which efficiency, in turn, has poured unbelievable wealth into the Pullman coffers. Pullman dividends are one of the six highest today. Lincoln's son, Robert, was for a long period, head of the Pullman Company; it is safe to say that whatever the Emancipator did for the Negro has been repaid, at least, to his son and the latter's company by members of the Negro group.

The Pullman Company goes to enormous expense in order to give good accommodation to the public, yet in the final analysis, it is the porter who is the medium through which that accommodation is handed to the public. Hence the porter really serves in the capacity on the train, second in importance only to that of the crew of the engine. In a certain aspect the porter is even more important than the latter, as he is in direct contact with the passenger, whose good-will is important to the Pullman Company. Good-will, it would be a truism to say, is the best promoter of business.

The detium of the long trip from New York to the Pacific Coast can be immensely relieved or heightened by the kind of porter one has, as perhaps every traveler knows. I have seen, again and again, the passengers on a car going to California, all like one happy, cheerful family, simply because of the example originally set by the porter. And I have seen the opposite, too, because the porter was a grouch and served as a wet blanket, a type, happily rare.

Intelligence, as was said, is one of the life's greatest assets. But that rule does not always hold. The educated porter, then as now, soon discovers if he does not know it intuitively and he usually does, that the more he dissimulates and lives up to the traditional character of "George," the better for his exchequer. What good would it be to belong to a "superior" race, if an "inferior" showed as much intelligence as you? Is not man superior to monkey because of intellect and Nordic Man to non-Nordic for the same reason? Catch any sane Nordic, or Negro for that matter, giving a "tip" to the destroyer of his pet theories. The simple formula for tip-getting is subserviency. More than once have porters lost a tip, after giving every other service, except that of laughing at some "nigger" joke.

As for myself when I had successfully placated the joke-teller, my diplomacy would sometimes fail, as there were other pit-falls. On one occasion while standing at a station in Iowa, a rooster from a nearby farm hopped near the train. A clever young New Yorker, on seeing it, at once caught me by the arm, and with the same degree of surprise as if the bird were a live pterodactyl, said:

"Hey, George, look! A chicken!"

Rising to the occasion I appeased the young fellow by registering as much surprise as if it were the first of its species I had ever seen. But I was soon to fall into another trap. A few minutes later while in the smoker resuming a conversation on English literature I had been having with a professor of that subject in a Western college, the young fellow walked in. After listening for a while, he tried repeatedly to swing the conversation back into the chicken and watermelon channel, evidently to save his face and from one of the friendliest passengers he finally became the most distant. And as to the tip rien du tout, as the French would say.

War, with government supervision of the railroads, brought a superficial change of conditions—superficial because while the porters got more wages it was also costing them more to live, and the passengers, on hearing of the increase, cut down the size of tips. Superficial, also, because the intelligent porter still fails to receive the proper recognition from the company. Both as to pay and hours of sleep there is a caste system, savoring of antebellum conditions, with the conductor, as the "White" overseer.

The Porter's Union

This article would be incomplete without mention of the effort being made by the more manly porters to remedy these injustices, and to get a living wage out of the immense profit that race prejudice has brought to the company. This effort, as is well known is the Brotherhood of Sleeping Car Porters, the Pullman Porters' Brotherhood, headed by A. Philip Randolph, who is assisted by an able and forward-thinking corps of men—incidentally Negroes—as I believe is to be found in any other American union today. Already, under the pressure of union-ism, the Pullman company has been making important concessions. It is further alleged that in its effort to defeat the Brotherhood, the Company has bought up the services of several Negro newspapers, whose names have been mentioned, and which have carried editorials favoring the company.

To those, who like myself, know and have felt Pullman conditions at their worst, the conduct of these newspapers seem positively heartless. I can recall, again and again, going from Chicago to California, a ride of 72 hours, running extra, with a full car, and absolutely no provision being made for my getting a minute's sleep, while the conductor, who sat around all day, turned in regularly around 2 a.m., if not earlier. I can recall being "cut out" many a time in some lone town in Montana desert, getting the sum total of a dollar a day or being "bawled" out by some petty agent of the company, after I had made a "hit" with the passengers, simply because he wanted to show authority. These incidents, sooner or later, had happened to perhaps every porter. Such conditions have been bettered somewhat only by unionization. If White men have been forced to form unions to get justice from White men, how much more imperative is such a step on the part of Negroes!

In the light of past experiences it is difficult for me to view opposers of this union other than as enemies of the Negro group. It is difficult to think of them other than as spiritual descendants of those "good" Negroes who were appointed slavedrivers, and got a hand-out from "massa" for their share in adding to the miseries of their fellow sufferers.

It is true that the Pullman Company has served man as a stepping-stone to better things, but it is difficult to see where any excessive gratitude is due. The question is: In employing Colored men, which did the company love better itself or the men? Could it have gotten the same combination of intelligence, subserviency, and thankfulness for the job from White men, would or would not that have affected the color of the men employed, as in the case of the conductor?

I hold no brief for the Brotherhood as such, but I feel that I do for the Negro group, and it is about time it uses its intelligence to enrich itself first, and then others.

NEGRO HOLDS HIGHEST POSITION UNDER FRENCH RULE, SAYS J. A. ROGERS

Mentions 5 In French Parliament And 1 In Senate; Also 1 Governor

Black Man Commanded a French Cruiser and Marshal Joffre Was Captain Under Black General

Pittsburgh Courier
October 1, 1927
J. A. Rogers

PARIS, Sept. 29—For some reason or other the Latin peoples have shown a tendency to treat Negroes less as inferior and more like human beings than the Anglo-Saxons. A notable instance: modern Negro slavery really began in Southern Europe when a lieutenant of Prince Henry the Navigator brought the first ten slaves from Guinea in 1442. Sixty years later with the discovery of the New World, Negro slavery was introduced in the West Indies by colonists from Spain.

Negro slavery was not abolished in Southern Europe until 1773, that is, it lasted for 351 years, yet to the best of my knowledge, there was at no time a color problem. On the contrary, Arurara, an eye witness of the arrival of the first batch of slaves, tells how they were taught trades, adopted into families and even married to "the women of the country." (See his "Chronicles," chapter 24 and 25.) Later all of those Negroes, hundreds of thousands of them, were absorbed—by the White population.

Although the Black man was brutally treated by all the White colonists in the New World, yet under the Latins the tendency above mentioned held true, with the result that they showed more manhood and perhaps higher intellectual advance than their fellow Negroes under Anglo-Saxon rule. At a time when slavery was at its worst, in the French Colonies, the Chevalier St. George, a Negro from Guadeloupe, noted swordsman, musician and composer of several operas was one of the leading personages at the court of Louis XVI. Henri Diaz, a Negro slave, was one of three, who won the independence of Brazil; Antonio Maceo was the leader of the Cuban revolt, while another Negro slave, whose name I shall mention at another time, was the George Washington of a leading North American country, and its president for several years.

It was under French rule that the individual Negro has made the highest advance. Under Napoleon, Gen. Dumas, commanded the French troops in Egypt, while Magloire Pelage, commanded a brigade in the Peninsular way under Marshal Soult. Gen. Alfred A. Dodds, another Negro recently dead, commanded the French troops during the Boxer Rebellion in China. He it was also who won much of France's African empire, Gen. Bonnier, under whom Joffre served as a captain, was in command at the capture of Timbuctoo, where he was killed.

Among the leading French Negroes at the present is M. Mortenol, former commandant of a French cruiser, who was in command of the aerial defense of Paris at Le Bourget during the War. Think of it, a Negro, and a dark one at that, holding this high post while our Colonel Charles A. Young, was sidetracked to Africa, evidently to keep him from well-earned promotion. I had two appointments with Commandant Mortenol. But was unable to keep them because of illness. I hope to say more about him later. Another dark Negro, Hector Simoneau, was prefect of the Department of Cantal, a position equivalent to that of governor of a state. M. Simoneau is now paymaster general of the Department of L'Aube. I was informed that an American general in command in the first-named department objected to taking orders from M. Simoneau, and that the French government shifted him to St. Malo.

There are six Negroes in the French Parliament, five in the Lower House, and one in the Senate—at least several persons have told me Senator Lemery, who is from Guadeloupe, is Colored. The other five are Deputies Delmont, Diagne, Severe, Jean Francois, and Candace. Deputy Candace, who has held and still holds important government positions, is a former professor of science in a French College. He is also a journalist and was editor of Clemenceau's famous paper, L'Action, as well as of other papers. He has been secretary to ex-Premier Viviani; and rapporteur-general on prisoners of war. A collaborateur of President Doumergue, he is interested in Colonia, Maritime and Finance. He has been a member of the Finance Committee seven years, vice-president of the Merchant Marine Committee; rapporteur on State Railways, and has been in Parliament 15 years.

Deputy Delmont is one of the foremost lawyers of Paris and has a very large practice. He was awarded both the Croix de Guerre and the Legion of Honor for his services during the war. Deputy Diagne, who also holds important posts under the government, represents Senegal. Of Deputy Diagne, I hope to say more later as illness also prevented my keeping interviews with him.

The presence of these Negroes in Parliament made it difficult for color prejudice to creep into France as has been shown more than once. Match these six deputies with the absence of Negroes in the British Parliament, England has a larger Black population than France. Among other leading Negroes are Louis Beaudza who is chief clerk of the Grand Chancellory of the Legion of Honor; Isaac Beton, professor of the Lycee St. Louis, Raoul Cenac, professor of the Lycee St. Michelet, (both government colleges); Col. Baibe, Intendant Militaire of the First Batt. Of Artillery, and a graduate of the Polytechnic School. Among the leading lawyers are Georges Mamerville, and Clanvile Bloncourt, both of whom have a large practice.

Camile St. Rose Fanchine, a young Negro of fine ambition, is a bookkeeper in a leading bank. M. Fanchine who, is much interested in the Negro, tells me that among other leading French Negroes must be added Admiral Amiot, retired Gen. Lecamus, killed in the last war, and Pellieres Lacournee, captain of a warship, and who was snubbed in a café in New York. M. Fanchine is winner of the Croix de Guerre.

M. Charles Louisade, 42 rue Monsieur Le Prince, former principal and inspector of schools in France, is in the real estate business, and owns a hotel and a restaurant. He thinks France offers a splendid field for Negro investors.

In an earlier article I told of my meeting with Monsier Germany, an inspector in the French Customs. I have also mentioned Benglia, the noted actor. And so one could go on to name others, near-Whites from the French West Indies, who in America would be known as Negroes, but space must be reserved for one whose fame is world-wide, Rene Maran, author of "Batouala." Maran, who served for 15 years in the French colonia service, is the voice crying in the wilderness. He thinks that France has been very unjust to the Black man, and "Batouala," as its readers know, is a stirring indictment of French colonial rule.

Maran is a humanitarian of the first rank, and a leading contributor to radical French journals. Another book of his has recently appeared "Djouma." As "Batouala," it has been translated into eight languages.

A word must be said in closing about the Negroes in the humbler walks of life. These may be encountered from time to time engaged in all kinds of occupations: driving an autobus, conducting a subway train, clerking in a department store, and generally in all work Negroes are rarely found in America.

In my next article I will endeavor to answer some of the questions asked me in the large number of letters I have received from Courier readers.

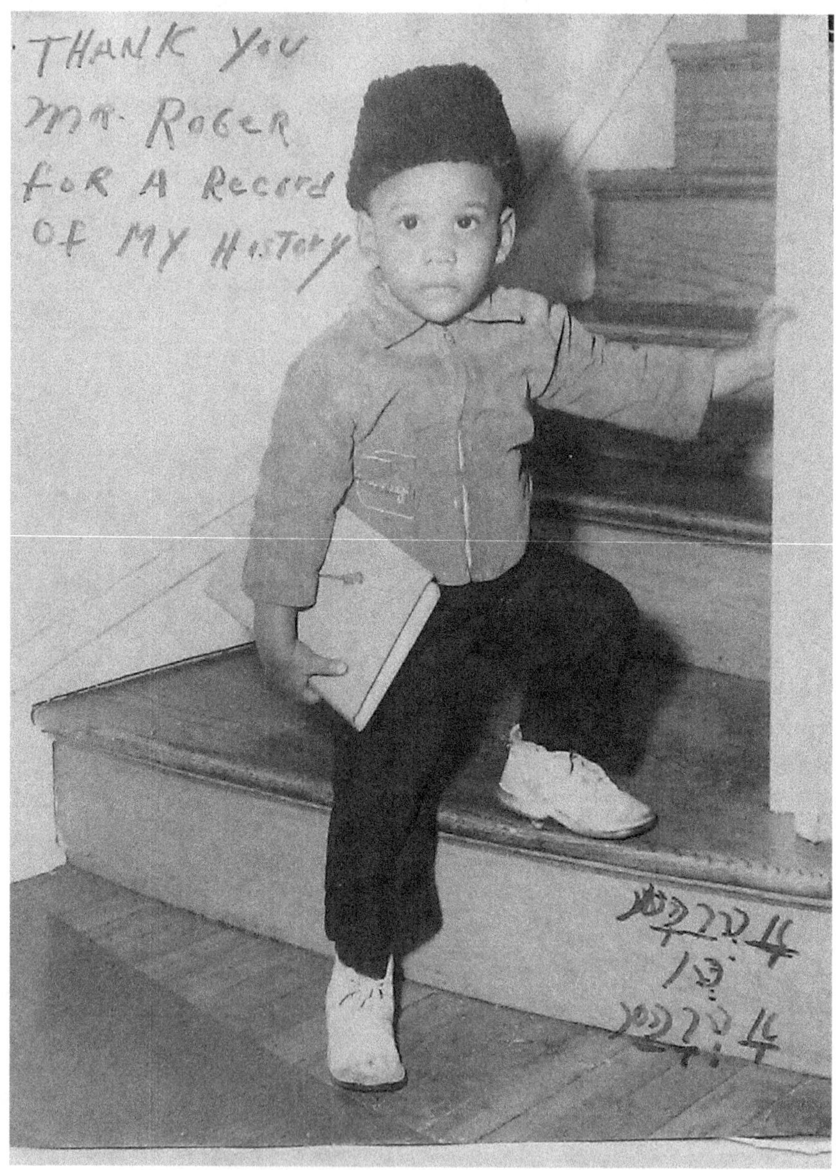

Image 3. Photo of Abraham Ben Abraham sent to Mr. J. A. Rogers as a token of appreciation for his work as a devoted Race Man.

Image 4. Photo of Mr. J. A. Rogers in Morocco, North Africa.

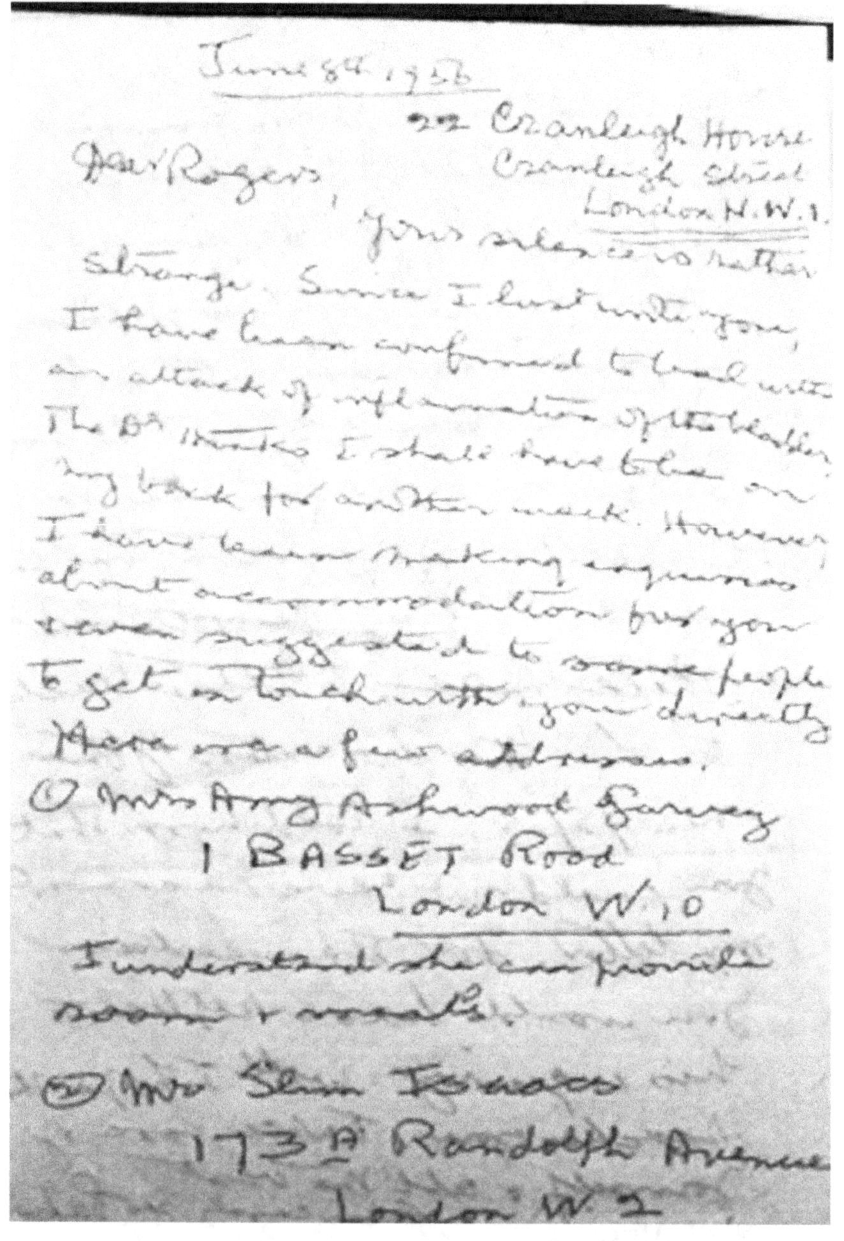

June 8th, 1956

22 Cranleigh House
Cranleigh Street
London N.W.1.

Dear Rogers,

Your silence is rather strange. Since I last wrote you, I have been confined to bed with an attack of inflammation of the bladder. The Dr thinks I shall have to be on my back for another week. However I have been making enquiries about accommodation for you & even suggested to some people to get in touch with you directly. Here are a few addresses.

(1) Mrs Amy Ashwood Garvey
1 BASSET Road
London W.10

I understand she can provide room & meals.

(2) Mr Slim Isaacs
173A Randolph Avenue
London W.2

Image 5A. A letter written to J. A. Rogers from George Padmore. Mr. Padmore recommends that Rogers contacts Marcus Garvey's first wife, Ms. Amy Ashwood Garvey who was living

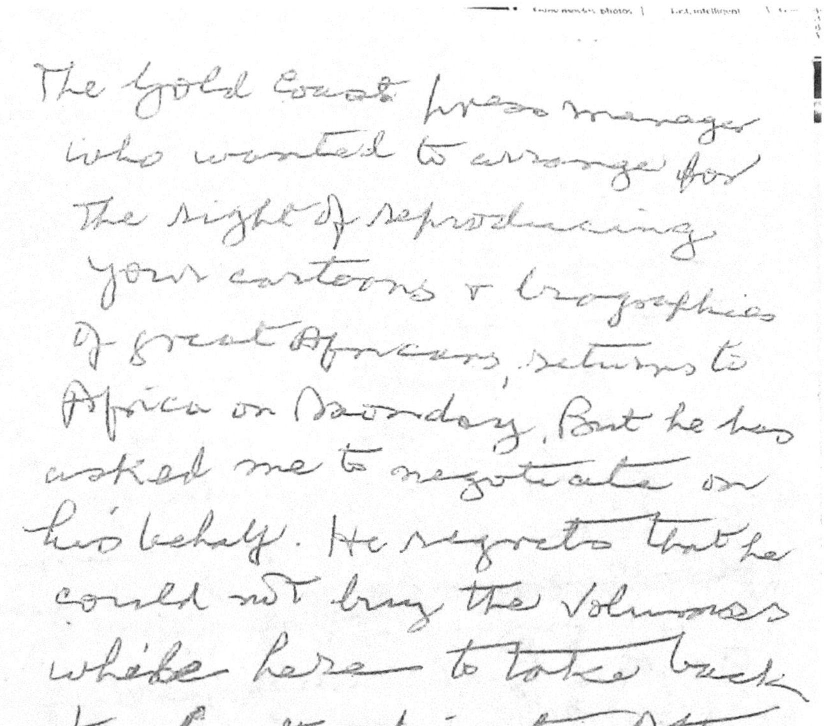

The Gold Coast press manager who wanted to arrange for the right of reproducing your cartoons & biographies of great Africans, returns to Africa on Monday. But he has asked me to negotiate on his behalf. He regrets that he could not buy the volumes while here to take back to show the directors of the newspaper. I told him that you could not have received my letter. For I am certain you would have replied to his enquiry. Well I hope this reaches you. Take care of yourself & all the best

Sincerely, Geo Padmore

Image 5B. (5A. continued) in London at the time. George Padmore, a former student of both Fisk and Howard Universities, left the United States and eventually moved to Accra, Ghana.

Image 6. J. A. Rogers in London.

26 Mar 57

Dearest Joel,

thanks for your letter of 21 Mar 57. Hope you got my various other letters plus my card from Bonn. I was awfully busy last week, part of the time on our projects here and part of the time on Mr. Lowrey's manuscript, but I wanted you to be happy, so I thought I might as well write often.

Those things I am buying here, I do not buy just for the sake of buying or spending money. That are things I like for us whether we do entertain much or not. As for silver and so on - it is so much cheaper here in Europe, same thing with china or cut glass, or table linen of the nicer variety. There is something like a well run household, - something I have right here, where I am on my own. I certainly don't intend not to have it the same way, when we are reunited. Since I come as a bride and bring things as a bride, I will NOT ~~to~~ have to pay customs on those things, only the shipping. It, therefore, is a material savings for us to bring things from here. BUT - I come from a business household myself, so I do understand that you have to be liquid for the books, and I probably would not have it otherwise. Yet on the other hand, though I am economically minded, I am not petty. Never in my life, I relished arguments on money - AND I NEVER WILL. It would have been nice, if I could have had the money, but as I made clear in my letter, only if it did not inconvenience you. I don't want any further arguments about it - just forget it. There might be said something more about it, but certainly not on paper.

I should hear from the consulate soon, if not, I will call them next Monday, and find out again as the girl told me I should. I hope it is clear, that when I know when I can come, that you will NOT repeat NOT send a ticket, but the money. It has been discussed here carefully. Apart from the fact, that I want to fly and not go by boat, I want to be able to fly with whatever company that has the first opening by then - but that are not all the considerations why the money is better than a possible ticket, but it is too technical to line it out to you on paper, just remember that that is the way that is best.

As regards the back room - I have my definite plans with it which we can discuss when I am with you. The main thing, as far as I am concerned is, that, if possible, you will be through with the painters in the house. I hate painters.

The weekend in Bonn was wonderful. Eberhard did everything to make it wonderful for me, since he wants me to remember it with fond memories. I have known him for a very long time. We did not see each other regularly, but every time we did see each other, it was, as if we never were apart from each other and with so divergent interests of our own, for any length of time. We discussed you and the prospects of getting to the States soon, but there is not much influence I have on the processing speed of the consulate.

I do miss you terribly, I do want to be with you as soon as I possibly can, I want to be in your arms and I want to be in your arms so badly that you don't know how badly. On the other hand, I am afraid of the change to the States and I at least want a household run in a cultivated European way. I do realize that you have been by yourself all your life, and that you are set in your ways. But please don't try to force all of them on me. I do want to make you happy with all my heart, but I expect to be happy too. And there are certain things that contribute to my happiness materially. And I do hate arguments or opinions forced on ~~my~~ me which are not my own.

I guess it would be better right now if I could be with you, right now, could kiss you and be kissed. I guess what is wrong with me too is that we are still separated. Lovingly Helga

Image 7. A letter to J. A. Rogers from his wife Mrs. Helga M. Rogers during a time when they were living apart.

Image 8. J. A. Rogers in Egypt, North Africa.

Image 9. (Left to Right) J. A. Rogers, Senator John F. Kennedy (D-MA), Cardinal Spellman, and Maryland Governor Theodore McKeldin at Waldorf, presenting Cardinal Spellman with the George Washington Carver award for 1956.

Image 10. J. A. Rogers visiting Morgan State University.

12 Mona Rd.
Kingston 6.
Jamaica, W.I.
Oct. 20, 64.

Dear Mr. Rogers;-

I understand that you have been assigned by "Negro Heritage" to write the biographical sketch on Marcus Garvey.

I got your address from the Consul General in New York, and mailed you a copy of the book- "Garvey & Garveyism" by book-mail, registered, ship on the 16th inst.,

I also enclose some clippings in connection with the proclamation of the Government that M.G. is the first NATIONAL HERO of Jamaican birth, and they are bringing his body back from England here on the 11th of next month, the State ceremony will be on Sunday the 15th, after this service he will be re-interred in the Mausoleum.

I trust you are well, and that life is not as strenuous as it was in the twenties.

I will be glad to answer any questions you may send me about M.G. and his work, so that your work will be accurate.

Best wishes,

Yours truly,

encls.

A. Jacques Garvey

Image 11. Letter from Mrs. Amy Jacques Garvey to J. A. Rogers.

Image 12. Envelope containing letter from Mrs. Garvey.

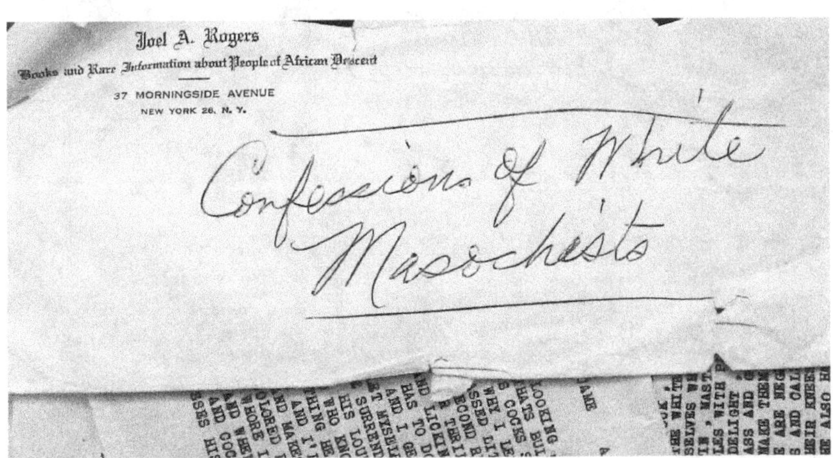

Image 13. While writing Sex and Race, J. A. Rogers received many letters from White people detailing their sexual behaviors and experiences with Blacks. The letter contained in this envelope was too vulgar and indecent to include in this book.

History is the foundation on which all progress of the individual or the group is laid.
The elephant, though much older and much stronger than man, is still a beast of burden after these millions of years because he has no concern in his history.

No. 1 — J. A. ROGERS' WEEKLY — 3 cents. By mail 5 cents. $1.50 a year

GEMS OF NEGRO HISTORY

The black man's history did not begin with slavery in Virginia. It goes back to the dawn of time.

By J. A. Rogers, traveller, historian, and Ethiopian war correspondent; author: "From Superman to Man," etc., etc. Illustrated by C. C. Bailey. Issued by J. A. Rogers Publications, 1845 Seventh Avenue, New York City.

ISABEAU,

A SHAPELY BLACK GIRL, WAS THE JOSEPHINE BAKER OF THE 1770'S. BORN A SLAVE IN THE FRENCH WEST INDIES, SHE INHERITED HER MASTER'S WEALTH AND WENT TO FRANCE WHERE SHE BECAME THE FAVORITE OF THE COUNT D'ARTOIS, LATER KING OF FRANCE. HER BEAUTY, CREATED MUCH JEALOUSY AMONG THE BEAUTIES AT VERSAILLES. THE FAMOUS MME. DUBARRY WROTE THAT THE ONLY HOPE OF THE WHITE BEAUTIES WOULD BE TO DYE THEIR SKIN BLACK LIKE ISABEAU'S...

DRAWING FROM PROF. CHURCHWARD'S CONCEPTION OF FIRST MAN

THE FIRST MASTERS OF THE EARTH!

THE EARLIEST KNOWN MEN WERE NEGROES WHO LIVED FROM 500,000 TO 2,000.000 B.C. ALMOST THE ONLY TRACES OF THEM ARE THEIR SKULLS WHICH HAVE BEEN FOUND ON THE FIVE CONTINENTS. LEADING SCIENTISTS SAY THAT THESE NEGROES WERE THE ANCESTORS OF THE WHITE RACE...

C. C. Bailey 37

TO DAY

DR. EMMETT J. SCOTT,

SECRETARY-TREASURER OF HOWARD UNIVERSITY, A PIONEER IN AFRAMERICAN EDUCATION. FAITHFUL COMRADE OF BOOKER T. WASHINGTON AND CO-WORKER IN THE BUILDING OF TUSKEGEE. SPECIAL ASST. TO THE SECRETARY OF WAR, 1917-19. NATIVE OF HOUSTON, TEXAS.

THE NEGRO TOUCHED UNITED STATES SOIL THE SAME DAY AS THE WHITE MAN. THE FIRST EUROPEAN ACTUALLY PROVED TO HAVE LANDED ON AMERICAN SOIL WAS PONCE DE LEON, MARCH 27, 1513, IN FLORIDA. WITH HIM AS OFFICER OF THE EXPEDITION CAME PEDRO MEXIA, A MULATTO.

QUESTION— IN WHAT WAY IS THE WEIGHING OF FINE GOLD AND DIAMONDS RELATED TO ANCIENT NEGRO HISTORY? (ANSWER NEXT WEEK)

NOTE. What is given on these leaflets is something more than "Negro" history; it is WORLD history featuring the black man just as all the other histories feature some particular race, nation, or group.

Image 14. J. A. Rogers' first "Gems of Negro History." A weekly publication issued by J. A. Rogers Publications.

THE READER'S DIGEST
PLEASANTVILLE · NEW YORK

January 12, 1961

Dear Mr. Rogers:

Thank you very much for sending along the manuscript entitled THE MOST UNFORGETTABLE CHARACTER I'VE MET. I think you have some interesting stuff on Haile Selassie but most of it is fairly familiar and has been covered in part in articles that we have run in the past. Also, the Unforgettable usually deals with a fairly close and intimate daily interrelationship between the writer and the character described.

I wish I could write you more favorably, particularly in view of your background and long standing interest in the African situation.

Sincerely,

Mr. J. A. Rogers
1270 Fifth Avenue
New York 29, N. Y.

Image 15. J. A. Rogers submitted a manuscript on Emperor Haile Selassie I of Ethiopia to The Reader's Digest entitled "The Most Unforgettable Character I've Met." It was rejected.

Image 16. J. A. Rogers in Egypt, North Africa.

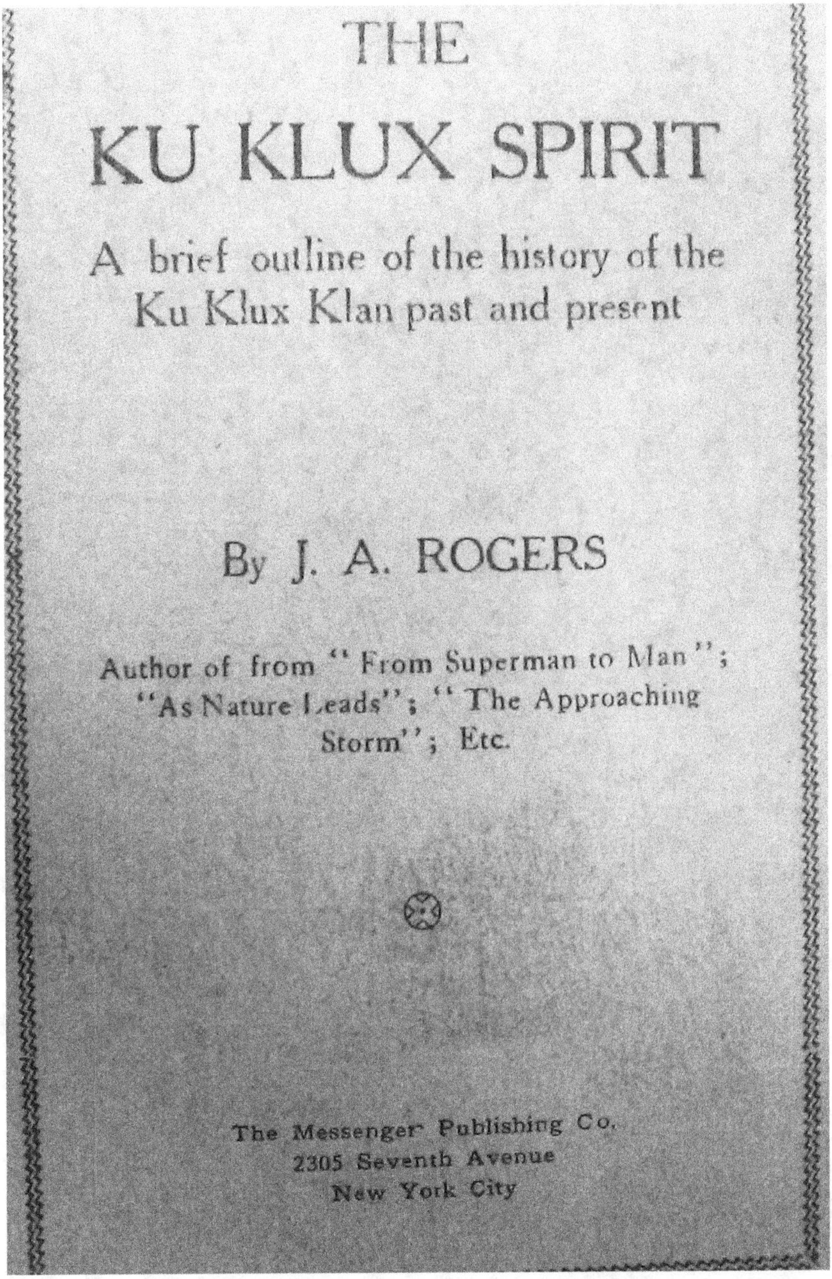

THE

KU KLUX SPIRIT

A brief outline of the history of the Ku Klux Klan past and present

By J. A. ROGERS

Author of from " From Superman to Man"; "As Nature Leads"; " The Approaching Storm"; Etc.

The Messenger Publishing Co.
2305 Seventh Avenue
New York City

Image 17. Cover page for J. A. Rogers' 1923 publication of The Ku Klux Spirit.

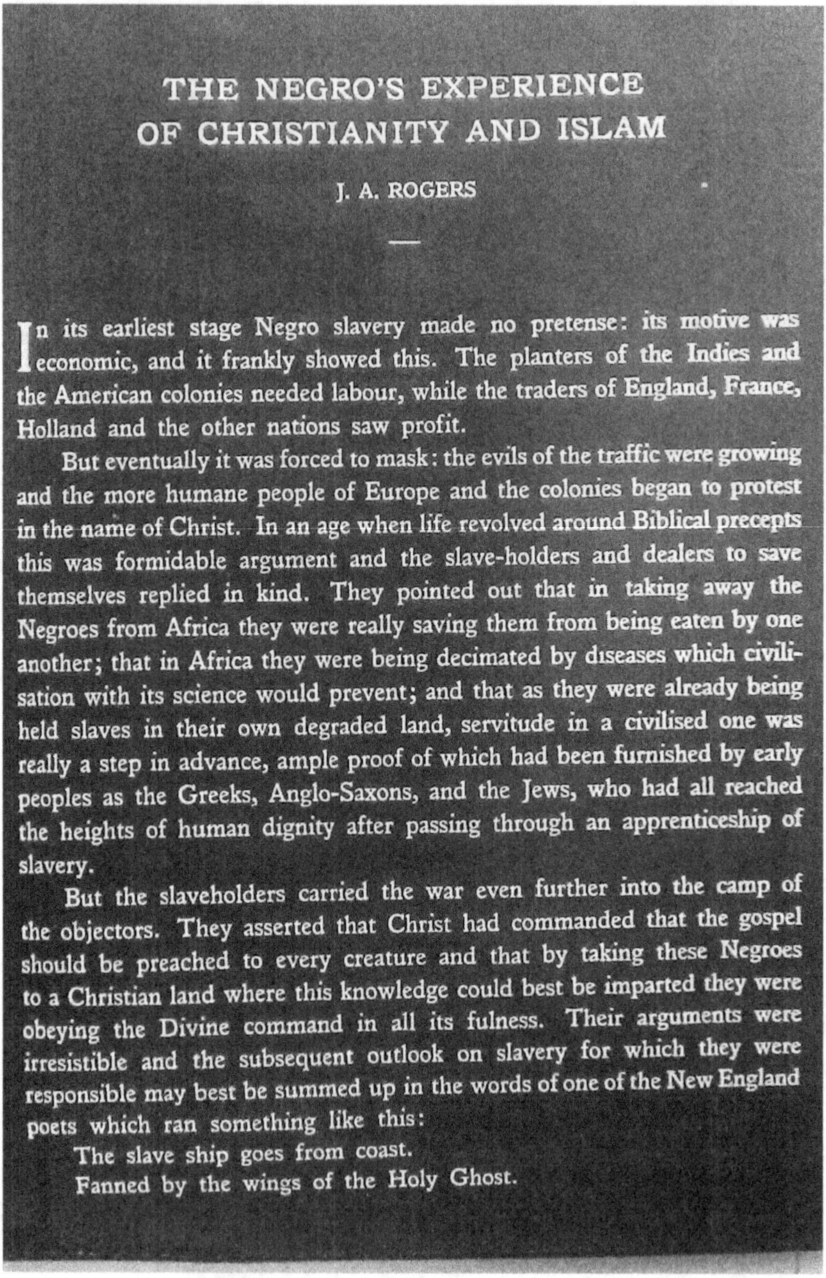

THE NEGRO'S EXPERIENCE OF CHRISTIANITY AND ISLAM

J. A. ROGERS

—

In its earliest stage Negro slavery made no pretense: its motive was economic, and it frankly showed this. The planters of the Indies and the American colonies needed labour, while the traders of England, France, Holland and the other nations saw profit.

But eventually it was forced to mask: the evils of the traffic were growing and the more humane people of Europe and the colonies began to protest in the name of Christ. In an age when life revolved around Biblical precepts this was formidable argument and the slave-holders and dealers to save themselves replied in kind. They pointed out that in taking away the Negroes from Africa they were really saving them from being eaten by one another; that in Africa they were being decimated by diseases which civilisation with its science would prevent; and that as they were already being held slaves in their own degraded land, servitude in a civilised one was really a step in advance, ample proof of which had been furnished by early peoples as the Greeks, Anglo-Saxons, and the Jews, who had all reached the heights of human dignity after passing through an apprenticeship of slavery.

But the slaveholders carried the war even further into the camp of the objectors. They asserted that Christ had commanded that the gospel should be preached to every creature and that by taking these Negroes to a Christian land where this knowledge could best be imparted they were obeying the Divine command in all its fulness. Their arguments were irresistible and the subsequent outlook on slavery for which they were responsible may best be summed up in the words of one of the New England poets which ran something like this:

The slave ship goes from coast.
Fanned by the wings of the Holy Ghost.

Image 18. Photo plate of an article written by J. A. Rogers on the impact of Islam and Christianity on American Africans.

XII. Left to right:Isis with the infant,Horus; centre:Diana of Ephesus,Greek,also known as the Goddess Multimammia,or Many-Breasted.Inset, enlarged to show Negroid face. Right,another conception of Isis and Horus. Below,Mylitta, greatest of the Assyrian goddesses.(See Notes on the Illustrations).

Image 19. A collage created by J. A. Rogers of various versions of the "Black Madonna" from civilizations pre-dating the Bible.

Ruminations

By J. A. ROGERS

1933

Introduces Dunbar To the Sorbonne

PARIS.—M. Louis T. Achille, instructor of French at Howard University, who is here on a leave of absence, recently presented to the graduate students in English at the Sorbonne a thesis on the "Life and Poetical Works of Paul Laurence Dunbar," which was enthusiastically received. The professors of the University, in particular, welcomed what is perhaps the first introduction of this great poet of Negro descent to the French public, and were warm in praise of it.

M. Achille

PART II

The following articles were found as newspaper clippings in the personal collection of J. A. Rogers held at Fisk University. There was no reference to which particular newspaper they came from, nor was a date found on the majority of the clippings (except in rare cases like the photo on the opposite page). It is the editor's belief that these clippings are actually from the New York Amsterdam News, in which Mr. Rogers wrote his famous "Rambling Ruminations" (also called "Ruminations") articles.

The reader will notice that these articles are much different than those presented in the previous section of this book. Mr. Rogers seems to be more direct in his confrontation of racist ideology and mis-information of Africa and her descendants. Although he maintains his almost comical approach to historical fact finding and the dispelling of myths, his disdain for deception is unmistakable.

Although these articles are relatively short, they are filled with morsels of information that could themselves, lead to other fine works by any researcher looking to enlighten themselves, the existing scholarship and literature. In true fashion, Mr. Rogers graced his readers with a glimpse into the world as seen through the eyes of a traveler and educator.

Rambling Ruminations

By J. A. ROGERS

Segregation and its Advocates

The question of segregation is in the air. Some, it appears, are advocating more of it. These are certainly gluttons, it seems to me, for if there is one thing we have nothing but in America it is segregation. Northwards of New York City as far as the Canadian border there is a certain degree of freedom it is true, but in all the vast region to the south and southwest there is enough of it to satisfy the most fire-breathing exponent of Negroism.

Who are the Negroes who advocate segregation and why do they do so? First, there are the leaders, who see more profit for themselves the more followers they have—in short, they're no different from the leaders of another -"ism," White or Black. Next there are the followers, who are animated with the mistaken notion that one way to cure the thing you are condemning in another group is to have more of it yourself. The psychology of these followers goes back ten thousand years, and differs not a whit in Black or White throughout the ages. I am convinced, therefore, that only sharpers or fools want segregation.

Sharpers or Fools

One has but to consider how segregation, in no matter what society or in what age, has always worked. In the case under consideration one finds that in all the things that make for the benefit of the dominant society the so-called Negro is a full-fledged citizen. Indeed in all the things that make for the national benefit, which in this case means largely White man's benefit—as say paying taxes, defending the nation, and the like—the Negro had better be a full citizen or he'll land in jail. On the other hand in nearly everything that makes for his own benefit he is a pariah, and were he to enforce too vigorously his demand for citizenship on this side, he would land in jail, also.

Exploiters All

Study the psychology of the advocates of segregation, White or Black and you'll find it identical. Both are exploiters, or would-be exploiters of their groups. Were it possible to change their present complexions each kind would readily fit into the opposite color. The great, great curse of the Negro has been his leaders, that is about 90 percent of them. Most of these spouters of catchy platitudes are endowed to an extraordinary degree with the gift of deluding the people, and themselves also, that they are talking for the masses, when all the time they are secretly looking out for their own petty, egotistical selves. Gandhi, working for the pariahs of India, lives like one of them. He travelled fourth class from India to England, which is horrible.

But the Negro followers are equally guilty as the leaders. First, they want to be amused and excited, and last of all to be instructed. Clowning and the desire to be clowned to is in our blood, put there I believe by the Whites, for the African Negro is dignified, if he is anything at all. Prospective Aframerican leaders ought first to take a course in vaudeville and monkey shines. The late Becton mastered this. In consequence we read that his loss was the great news of Aframerica in 1933.

Social Equality

Our great task is to break down segregation. In all those things that are degrading so-called social equality has been forced on us. We must demand social equality in the elevating things. Jimcrowism must be replaced by the freedom to enter public places; concubinage by legal marriage; and the back-door entrance to life be made to give way to the front door one.

We must demand citizenship and cease being like the White convicts on parole, the only other ones in America, besides us, whose movements are restricted to any appreciable degree.

In the meantime equally important is the task of self-development. We need first modern knowledge in the current ways of making a living, and next about our own history. This latter is to serve not for a boast, but as a driving force for the former. Slavery and the degradation forced unto us can be overcome by the inspiration derived from knowledge of our past. The Germans in the Eighteenth Century were far below the present level of Aframerican. In some parts as Westphalia they were actual slaves in a far more degraded condition than the Negro slaves of their time. Yet before 1914 Germany was the foremost intellectual country of the world and the best developed in most ways. The Germans had high-souled, unselfish leaders, however. And when Aframerica is ready for such leaders, it will also take its place in the sun.

Rambling Ruminations

By J. A. ROGERS

Compares Lynching With Nazi Outrages

E. Haldeman-Julius, publisher of the Little Blue Books, who usually strikes the bull's-eye on almost every question, compares Jewish persecution in Germany and lynching of Negroes in America in the *American Freeman* for September, 1934. He says:

"The cases are not similar at all. Lynchings in the United States are committed by the lowest elements of our inhabitants in sections that are notoriously backward...These lynchings are not provoked by our Federal or State governments. The White House does not conduct a lynch propaganda. Congress has passed no laws authorizing the lynching of Negroes. The Supreme Court has never said that lynchings are legal. Our philosophers have never outlined a theory justifying racial persecution...

"In Germany, on the other hand, racial persecution is part of a nation's law. Hitler has made racial persecution a perfectly legal procedure. The courts defend such behavior. The professors write 'learned' books on the necessity for racial persecution. The powers of the state are used to provoke acts of discrimination and violence against racial minorities."

Word Juggling

This is mere juggling with words, and had it been some other question, Haldeman-Julius, himself, would have been among the first to call it that. The barbarous Nazis openly declare that the Jew is not their equal and promptly proceed to treat him as such. Good, moral, Christian America writes in her Constitution that the so-called Negro is an equal, and then proceeds to treat him far more barbarously than the most barbarous Nazi has ever treated a Jew. The treatment of the Jew in Germany—and this is no attempt to condone it—has been greatly exaggerated by certain Jewish editors and leaders on this side with an eye to circulation and the collection plate.

Americans More Barbarous

The Nazis, so far, have yet to take a Jew, unsex him, and toss the gruesome objects to the women and children in the crowd, or to burn a Jew alive and drag his charred remains through the town. Hitler would be the first to oppose that. Europe and the German people, themselves, would never stand for that. They have not yet sunk so low. When it comes to real downright savagery the Nazis will have to come to America for lessons.

Haldeman-Julius is quite wrong when he says lynching is confined to backward communities. Certainly Duluth, Omaha, Springfield, Ill., Chicago and Atlanta, where Negroes have been lynched in recent years, cannot be called such. The Supreme Court, the White House and the State and Federal governments, it is true, have never advocated lynching, but what is just as bad or worse than the Nazis they have done nothing to prevent it though it is their sworn duty to do so. Were it dogs that were being lynched in America, the Christian churches which are so anxious to make America good and moral in every other respect would have raised such a howl that the forces of law from the White House downwards would get busy at once to stop it.

Begins At The Top

Further, lynching has been openly advocated on the floors of Congress, which, moreover, has resolutely refused to pass a law making it illegal. One turns in vain the darkest pages of history for a parallel to this. Contrary to Haldeman-Julius, American philosophers by the scores have written in justification of racial persecution, among them no less a one than the great Lester F. Ward. The Federal Government itself, in direct violation of the document from which it derives its authority, has evolved a philosophy of racial discrimination and practices it. Lynching in America begins at the top. It begins in the Federal and State governments, the churches, the universities and centers of culture, and works its way downwards. The lynchers are merely carrying out what many of the upper classes feel, and perhaps would like to do themselves. The lynchers are but bouncers of Nordic superiority. Since they are left free to work their will, they derive their authority from on high as effectively as the Nazis get theirs from Hitler.

Rambling Ruminations

By J. A. ROGERS

Kid Cupid and Jack Johnson

(PARIS – 1933)

Jack Johnson, whose encounters with Cupid proved far more deadly for him than the most formidable fighters of his day, has been writing his memories for L'Intransigeant, leading every evening paper of this city. On the day of my arrival here there appeared the nineteenth installment, in which he tells of his marital bouts. His fourth marriage, the preceding three which had been to White women, brought down even more severe criticism on him, he says, the more so as this last wife was young and beautiful while his life had been "fertile in catastrophe."

But, says Jack, he has found happiness at last; he and his wife, Irene Pinau, after eight years, love each other as much as on the day they met, and that after having considered the obstacles against intermarriage, he is more than ever in favor of it.

"I know well," he says, "that the question has often been raised: Can a White woman married to a Colored man be happy? In America, especially, where color prejudice is unshakably anchored, when a White woman marries a Black man she runs the risk of being renounced by her parents, her friends and by all of her race. She is forced to live in the Negro neighborhood, where she meets with little or no sympathy from the Colored women. After all of this, ought not such unions be invariably unhappy?"

Race Doesn't Count, He Says

"Irene and I do not think so. The question of race matters little. Everything depends upon the character of the couple. Do not a great number of marriages between people of the same color end in divorce after years of infernal discord?"

Speaking as an authority on both sides of the fence, Jack declares that it doesn't matter whether one's wife is Colored or White, if a pair is not harmoniously matched in temperament, discord will come sooner or later. "On the other hand," he says, "when two human beings entertain a mutual and equal affection for each other, when they are happy to make the innumerable little concessions one to the other that marital life demands, their union, regardless of color, will be filled with joy, and all regret will be excluded."

Decided He Wanted White Women Only

Jack, whose fistic courage, sunny disposition and kindliness are admired by even his worst enemies, has evidently learned wisdom with the years and the misfortune they brought him. He began with Negro women but, having had no luck with them, he decided, as he says in his autobiography, which was published some years ago, "to forswear Colored women and to determine that my lot henceforth would be cast only with White women." But the fact is it was a change that brought him actual ruin. While the Colored women used whips, the White ones wielded scorpions. According to his own confession he has seen that a change of skin-color in the objects of his affection did not make life easier for him, but that it is mutual affection and self-sacrifice which are the essentials for a harmonious love-life, and not color.

With a little more patience and discernment of the women of his own group (for it was Jack's fault why he so often picked the wrong women, White and Black), this greatest boxer the world has ever seen, instead of being now a shadow of his former self, might be a figure of importance, financial and otherwise. His decision was fatal, even while admitting the natural and inherent right of Johnson or any other individual to marry whom they please, regardless of color.

Reflecting further, Johnson's decision to marry White was deliberate, like that [of] some of those superior folks, White and Colored, who decided to deal no further with Negroes, because one or two of that group with whom they had dealings did not come up to expectancies. It was also probably due to that inferiority complex, which is common among those who have come up from the bottom, regardless of color. The daughter of the rich American pork-packer, or the White movie star whose mother was a washer woman, must need to compensate for their low social origin by marrying some effete European nobleman, so-called. Englishmen, generally, regard the American as an inferior creature, and to win English social esteem rich White Americans of a democracy will send their daughters across the Atlantic, thousands of miles, to curtsey to King George and Queen Mary. To realize fully what this means, imagine members of the English aristocracy sending their daughters to the White House to make obeisance to the First Lady of the Land! Similarly—and we must face the facts—the marriage of many a Black man to a White woman, or the refusal of many Negroes who are rich, professional or otherwise influential to patronize Negro business is due largely to a desire to curry favor with those they believe of a superior caste.

The Call Of Color

Of course, there is also a certain attraction of "race" which, I am convinced after long years of study and research, is almost purely natural in the case of the White towards the Black, but almost wholly artificial in the case of the Black towards the White. That is, White is attracted to Black for natural causes, while Black is drawn towards White largely for social glamour.

Even now Colored Montmartre is witnessing the love affair of the daughter of a very rich, powerful and influential Southerner with a humble Negro musician. Her whole training has been directed against this sort of thing. In her native state the Negro would have been lynched for even daring to accost her. White men, from Presidents of the United States downwards, have also forsaken, periodically at least, their White mates for the Black daughters of Eve in order to satisfy some craving of the soul.

What are those qualities within the so-called Negro group that have pulled these rich and powerful Whites of both sexes towards it in spite of all social training and tradition? Suppose the so-called Negroes try to discover what these qualities are? Nothing is to be gained in trying to sidestep the group with which Destiny has identified us. The real progress of the so-called Negro will not begin until he starts on a voyage of discovery of himself.

Rambling Ruminations

By J. A. ROGERS

The Color Line in Merrie England

The four Mills Brothers and their company are reported as having been barred from the London hotels. The same happened to Roland Hayes, Paul Robeson, Marcus Garvey, Robert S. Abbott and others. The unpleasant fact is that while the lighter-Colored Negroes are accepted almost anywhere in England, the darker ones, including dark Hindus, are usually barred.

England is the only country in Europe where this condition exists. On the continent the darkest man may walk boldly into even the most luxurious palace of Cytherea, and be accepted. I have yet to learn of a single instance where a Negro was barred in Europe, except to please White Americans, and that is rare.

Origin Of Prejudice

Color prejudice, to the best of my knowledge, originated among the English-speaking peoples, and is almost their monopoly. In South American countries, and in certain French and Portuguese colonies in Africa, there is a mild form of it, but it thrives best only in English-speaking lands.

Now explain this? Negro slavery began in England and Portugal about the same time, 1440 , and this had its parallel in emancipation, 1773. But what a difference. In Portugal the Negro rapidly became a power, and Negroes even mounted the throne there. But as late as 1731 one finds a Jim Crow law in London, barring the Blacks from learning trades.

Shakespeare and Slavery

Shakespeare lived during Negro slavery in England. In injecting color prejudice into "Othello" he was therefore really using his English experiences. It is very doubtful whether color would have caused any objection to Othello's union with Desdemona on the European continent. Historical instances to the contrary are many. Charles V, one of the most powerful rulers of all European rulers, married his only daughter to a Mulatto, himself head of the most illustrious royal family of Europe at that time.

The color problem, now becoming world-wide, really began in Virginia in 1619 with the introduction of Negro slavery. In the West Indies and South America a hard and fast color line was impossible. Exception was nearly always made in the case of the Mulattoes, as the Whites, being few in number, needed these to bolster up their system of exploitation. But in the United States the Whites existed in such large numbers that they did not need the Mulatto, and thus arose the Anglo-American dictum that one "drop" of African strain made one a Negro. But after the abolition of slavery mixed marriages became legal in Virginia—that is, for Octoroons to marry White. A similar thing is true in South Carolina and certain other states now. But nowhere else, however, did the color bar become as rigid as in the United States, not even in Cape Colony. The South Africa Yearbook shows, as far as I can remember, more than a thousand legal mixed marriages in South Africa in the last few years. One of these was that of an English nobleman, Lord Grey, to an ordinary Hottentot woman.

Negroes Partly To Blame

In my historical researches I have found that color prejudice in England is centuries old. Nevertheless this English color line was never strong, though it is a British rule to treat natives inferior to subjects of the Mother Country and such

Whites as Canadians, etc. The English people, however, are polite—the politest I know. Hence, I am inclined to think that a certain type of Negroes in the British Isles had much to do with the growth of modern color prejudice there. Under Victoria and Edward VII there was practically none. During the war, however, Negroes were taken in large numbers to work in factories, and later in the struggle for jobs, race riots broke out in England precisely as in America. Because of the difficulty in making a living in England many Negroes are forced to do objectionable things.

Rambling Ruminations

By J. A. ROGERS

Return Of Old Time American Justice

Good old-time American "Justice" returned with a bang this week when Judge S. F. Davis of Greenwood, Miss., sentenced O. C. Brown to death for the alleged theft of $1.85. The sole difference between a sentence of that kind now and a century ago is that it was White people, not Negroes who used to get it. Negroes then were valuable property, while the poor Whites were worth, under the law, just what the Negroes now are.

Brown, it appears, had been short-changed $4.95 by an Italian peddler named Fiume. When Fiume refused to pay. Brown sought him out later with a gun and forced the Italian to hand over $1.85 in cash and the remainder of the $4.95 in goods. He was charged with robbery with firearms. Brown, incidentally, shot in the knee a deputy sheriff who intervened in the argument between him and the Italian, but he was not tried on this far more serious charge, since wounding carries only a prison sentence.

In colonial days, and even later, as one may read in McMaster's history, or any other record of those times, people were hanged for stealing even such trivial things as flour. A White man who stole a pig went to the gallows for sure. The Negro thief was also sentenced to death, but he usually escaped, unless he was free. A slave's value and that of the article stolen were compared, with the result that it was thought the height of all that was ridiculous to destroy an article worth several hundreds of dollars for another worth less than a dollar. Sufficient reason, as Schopenhaur would say, was always found why the Black man should not hang. The poor White, worth nothing, had nothing in his favor.

With the emancipation, the overlords shifted their tactics. The poor Whites and the slaves changed places so far as their value was concerned. The ex-slaveholders, disarmed now, needed the poor White to keep the freedman in a state of subjugation where his labor could be had at a slave wage. Formerly, when these poor Whites attempted to lynch a Negro, they were shot down like wolves for destroying property. But after emancipation the more Negroes they lynched the better, as that cowed the Negroes and made them thankful for small mercies.

Surely, all of this makes very clear the economic basis of our laws and our society and, for that matter, all human society. Yet the vast majority of Aframericans, the chief victims of capitalist laws, continue to reason sentimentally. Since the business of life is to live and to get the most possible out of it, and since money is the most powerful thing in our civilization, it seems to me that we ought to reason economically first also. Everything has an economic base—religion, science, poetry, art. Take money away from any of these things and it is like pulling the skeleton out of a man. Why continue putting the cart before the horse?

What most Negroes need is a very strong injection of skepticism. For the past thirty years I have been throwing overboard the old ideals injected into us when we couldn't help ourselves, and I find I have a lot yet more to throw out if ever I am to stop living in a fool's paradise, and quit being a tool of someone else. Most of us are scared of a little physical constipation. But what about mental constipation, which is just as bad in its own way?

The case of Brown is a very ordinary occurrence south of the Mason-Dixon Line. And yet so many of us glibly talk about Lincoln freeing the slaves. The nominal emancipation helped some, but it made it a darn sight worse for millions. And conditions will never be improved until first we think economically.

A law against lynching is soon to be introduced in Congress. We hope that some strong provision will be made against legal lynching, which is far more to be feared than lynching by a mob. For every Negro lynched by a mob there are a hundred lynched by a judge and jury.

Rambling Ruminations

By J. A. ROGERS

Black Officers Under Napoleon

Of Napoleon, France's greatest hero, thousands of books have been written. As Hannibal is the greatest genius of war in ancient times, so is Napoleon in our day. Even now the story of his life is being filmed at Hollywood. We wager, however, that nothing likewise will be said of the role played by Negroes in the career of the great Corsican.

And that role was of first-rate importance. Elsewhere we have given the names of eleven of his Negro generals, all of whom were born in Haiti or Guadeloupe, and commanded armies or brigades in France. The greatest of these was General Alexander Dumas, father of the great novelist and who was Napoleon's superior officer for several years. Dumas it was who really paved the way for him. Indeed, it was only by a strange twist of fate—sheer luck, as it were—that Napoleon was made head of the French army over Dumas, who was the senior general.

Of that Negro who helped Napoleon to fame and fortune still less is ever said. This was a Black Cuban giant named Joseph Damingue, better known as Hercules. The crucial battle of Napoleon's early career was that of Arcole, and it was practically Damingue who won that engagement.

Napoleon wrote: "I ordered Citizen Hercules, officer of my guides, to choose twenty-five men of his company to follow the course of the Adige for a mile and a half and then to charge at a grand gallop upon the rear of the enemy, sounding several trumpets. This manoeuvre succeeded perfectly; the infantry of the enemy was shaken by it." After this Napoleon attacked and won a comparatively easy victory.

To each guide Napoleon gave 72 francs; to each general, save one, 1,000 pounds, and that one received 2, 000 pounds, while to Damingue he gave 20,000 pounds, about $80,000. Further Napoleon thought so highly of the services that Damingue had rendered at this battle that he made him a captain, and of the 100 swords distributed to the bravest of the brave in his army, Damingue received one which was engraved: "For having overthrown at the head of 25 guides an Austrian column at the battle of Arcole."

At another battle, with a handful of men, Hercules threw himself upon two Croat battalions that formed the rear-guard of the Austrian army and forced them to surrender.

He went to Egypt with Napoleon and, at the Battles of the Pyramid and Aboukir, fought with his usual valor. In this latter engagement, when sent by Napoleon to capture a redoubt, he swept beyond it and took all the enemy's trenches. Napoleon reproached him for having exceeding his orders, at which he replied: "How could I help it. We were in such an easy road." For this exploit Napoleon made him a major, and as such he commanded, side by side, in the Chasseurs of the Mounted Guards, with the Prince Eugene, Napoleon's stepson, for the next three years.

But, alas for Damingue, who aspired to be a marshal of France, he could neither read nor write, which made him increasingly unfit not only for promotion but even for his present rank. The Empire had grown stronger; it had become established.

Hercules Garners Highest Decorations

So far as decorations were concerned, Damingue had received the highest of them. He wore the Golden Eagle, and he had been one of the first to receive the Legion of Honor. Napoleon, not wishing to turn off one who had done so much for him, gave him command of a Black battalion. But Hercules, who had so long commanded White men, was disgusted at this and left the army. Napoleon, however, gave him full pay as a pension.

Retiring to Italy, he lived at Monza, where he married a Milanese woman, by whom he had two children. In 1816, after the overthrow of Napoleon, of whom he had become a great enemy, he returned to France and entered the service of Louis XVIII, who made him aide-de-camp to General de Fontanges on the latter's mission to Haiti, with the title of major-general, retired.

Hercules used to assert that Napoleon, embarrassed over the injustice of his non-promotion, used to send him later into the most dangerous part of the battle, hoping that he would be killed. In his old age Hercules loved to relate how he, a son of Cuba, coming to Fontanges, first engaged, while a boy, as a drummer, and had won the drum-sticks of honor, before the Revolution.

Surely, the stirring story of this valiant Black giant would give striking color and incident to the picture of Napoleon now being made. Will it and that of any of the other Negroes who contributed to Napoleon's success be included? Had they been clowns, crap-shooters and gin-bibbers, instead of heroes who commanded White men, it is safer to predict that they would be.

* * *

For those who are interested in knowing more of the Negro's role in history I take the opportunity to say that I am giving a series of talks on "Great Negroes," and will continue for the next few Sundays at 3 p.m. in the Little Theatre of the Y. M. C. A. Among the personages yet to be treated are: Gen. Alexander Petion, called the George Washington of Haiti; Naval

Captain Mortenol, who commanded the Air Defenses of Paris in the last war, and Ira Aldridge, foremost Shakespearean actor of his time.

Rambling Ruminations

By J. A. ROGERS

Mob Rule Places America In Bad Light

Last week there happened an international incident which, though given little newspaper space, had far-reaching implications.

When Eastern Maryland and the San Jose lynchings occurred the European newspapers gave them front-page publicity. In England one enterprising movie-firm re-enacted the lynchings and the driving of the Negroes from an Eastern Maryland town for their weekly news events.

All of this coming on top of the Scottsboro case was bad advertisement for America, hence diplomatic wires were at once pulled and the picture was withdrawn.

The United States, of course, desires to be known abroad as the shepherd of democracy and the champion of human rights. At the League of Nations America has been assigned to the task of protecting the Jews made homeless by bad wolf, Hitler. James G. McDonald of New York, who has been appointed high commissioner of the Jewish refugee problem, and Dr. J. P. Chamberlain, the American delegate, were, therefore, to say the least, placed in an embarrassing position by the news of Negro refugees in America. Indeed, the situation is strongly reminiscent of the fable of the shepherds and the wolf from Aesop.

A wolf, says Aesop, peering through the window of a hut, saw to his great surprise some shepherds devouring a roasted sheep, on which the wolf observed: Gentlemen, suppose you had ever caught me doing that?

U. S. Grew Angry Over Russian Lynchings

The American mind, as regards the Negro, reminds one of those shepherds. Under President Taft, for instance, while lynching in America was at its worst, the United States broke off diplomatic relations with the bad wolf, Russia, because the Jews were being lynched in that land. The same attitude has been true since.

Happily for the Negro, however, color atrocities are viewed abroad as atrocities abroad are viewed here. Outside of the United States, lynching is regarded as what President Roosevelt has just said it is: mass murder. Now among all peoples the murderer is abhorred because he gives us all a feeling of unsafety. The plain inference abroad is that the country in which these mass murders are permitted lacks law and order, for while we at home think of Maryland or San Francisco as the guilty place, those in other lands think of it as America. The result is that American business and prestige suffer.

At present there is great commercial rivalry among the nations, and since, as we said, the murderer is universally abhorred, America's business rivals abroad play up these lynchings, just as the North, although she had little or no love for the Negro, played up the injustices of slavery in the South to stir public opinion against the latter during the Civil War. The agitation waged by the North against the South finally won over even England, who was dependent on Southern cotton.

Rambling Ruminations

By J. A. ROGERS

Enslavement of Whites in Africa.

Much has been written on the African slave trade and very much more is destined to be, for this unpeopling of one continent to populate another is one of the most amazing chapters in human history.

Nothing like it had ever happened before. It is true that from the days of the Pharaohs onwards through the Carthaginians, the Moors, the so-called Barbary pirates, down to 1815 when the United States navy under Commodore Decatur entered the Mediterranean and broke up the enslavement of White Americans by Africans, millions, perhaps, of White Europeans had been taken into Africa, where their Mulatto descendants are to be found to this day, especially in North Africa.

That is to say, the capture of Europeans by Africans for enslavement began long before that of Africans by the Europeans and ended almost at the same time - a period of 3,000 years.

But the difference is this: Though the African slave trade lasted only 400 years (from 1442 when the Negroes were taken to southern Europe, and from 1502 when they were first brought to the New World, down to about 1830) the deportation of the African was far more systematic. It is probable that the number of White people enslaved by the Negroid peoples of Africa during this long period was far greater than the Negroes brought to America, but it was the very shortness of the period and the intensity which it was pursued that made the slave trade so deadly to Africa—so ruined African civilization that it continued to exist a shadow of its former self, like one who has been gassed.

One of the latest books on this subject is by Charles de la Ronciere, former president of the French Academy of Marine, and is entitled "Negres et Negriers (Negro Slaves and Slaveships)." There are many books more voluminous than that by M. de la Ronciere, but few, if any, are more engrossing; and still fewer, if any, contain the rarity of information, which is authentic since it is taken direct from the logs of ships and from the writings of those who were engaged in the slave traffic.

Space will not permit a review of this, on the whole, excellent work; therefore, only some of the little known items of information will be given here, especially as we find traces of them in so-called race relations today. On the slave ships where cruelties beyond the power of description were inflicted on the captives, and while they yet understood no language but their own, they were made to listen to prayers and the reading of the Bible three times a day before their wretched meals. This was to inspire them with "respect for the Supreme Being," all with the object of rendering them submissive when they arrived in the New World. Here, as is known, whatever else was deprived them, religion never was. Care, however, was taken in North American colonies to see that they never learned to read the Bible, because that would mean the ability to read other matter.

Slavers Practiced Terrible Cruelties

Certain of the captives went on a hunger strike, and the slavers at the prospect of losing these whipped them mercilessly to make them eat, and "if they persisted they were beaten with bars of iron; legs and arms were broken, and their frightful cries dissuaded others from following their example."

Sometimes the captives leaped off in scores into the sea, or otherwise took their lives. To overcome this longing for home and liberty they were twice a day forced to dance about on deck, the chains on their arms and legs keeping time with the drum and the African chant. Woe to those who did not sing and dance. "The whip would whistle over this circle of human cattle, forcing it through terror to give itself up to laughter and joy. This laughter, so necessary to the health of the captive, the slavers would sometimes try to induce by painting themselves white and yellow and doing all kinds of monkey tricks."

It was at night that the Negroes would commit suicide by swallowing their tongues or anything else they could get; therefore it was then that the slavers had to be on guard. These Blacks were in mortal fear; they believed that they were being taken to America to be eaten by the Whites, their bones ground to make gunpowder, and their skins used for shoes. One is reminded here of one captive, who later became a peer of the British realm, Bishop Crowther. Crowther, whose native name was Adjai, was taken from a slave ship that had been captured by a British warship. Taken aboard the warship Adjai said he felt that he was going to be eaten, as the first thing he saw there was a side of newly-killed pork, the color of which was so strikingly like that of his rescuers that he was sure they were in the habit of eating one another.

Captives Revolted and Slew Captors

In spite of all precautions the captives sometimes broke loose and terrible was their vengeance, as in the case of those on the Amistad, who killed all their captors and brought the vessel to port. On the Samuel Marie, for instance, the captives revolted and seizing pulleys, bits of iron and wood, used them as projectiles in a furious battle. "The carnage was terrible, and when the Blacks found at last that they could not overcome the Whites, they killed each other or jumped into the sea."

There was also the revolt on the French ship Avrillon of 500 Yolofs. When the slavers freed some of them for work on shipboard they killed the captain and others and overran the ship. The revolt, however, was subdued by the Whites, who, armed with rifles and cannon, picked off the rebels from behind barricades. Two hundred and thirty dead or dying Negroes were later thrown into the sea.

When on another ship the captives were suspected of revolt, one woman was hung up from a mast and one hundred pieces of flesh cut from her body, leaving bare the bone, while another had the liver, the heart and entrails torn out before the other captives, after which the flesh was cut into small pieces, and each made to eat of them.

Negroes As Bad As Whites in Cruelty

All in all, it is a horrible, but alas true, recital of man's inhumanity to man. There was nothing racial about it, for it was the Negro kings and chiefs who were the most active procurers of these slaves, often for the most trivial considerations. Some of them were as eager to sell their own flesh and blood as some English people were to sell their offspring into slavery in the American colonies in the seventeenth century, which latter practice caused Parliament to inflict the punishment of death without benefit of clergy on the offenders.

The treatment of the White slaves by Black kings of Africa was equally horrible. One of these, Mulai Ismail (Emperor of Morocco, whose portrait may be seen in "World's Greatest Men of African Descent" by J. A. Rogers), had 25,000 White slaves to build his city of Meknes. Voltaire in "Candide" tells of some of these cruelties on captured Whites by Black sea-rovers, among them that of the daughter of a Pope and an Italian princess. This woman of exquisite beauty was captured by a Moroccan Negro captain.

Rambling Ruminations

By J. A. ROGERS

The Basis of Race Prejudice

Certain few Aframerican writers and thinkers have long insisted that color prejudice is the result not so much of badness of heart in White people as of their non-acquaintance with the true facts about the so-called Negro.

What seems to be definite proof of this has been offered by Dr. Paul W. Schlorff as the result of a study he made for his doctor's thesis at the School of Education of New York University. Dr. Schlorff questioned 425 White high school students, composed principally of foreign-born parentage - Irish, Jewish, Italian, German - as to which of the many groups composing this nation they thought the most desirable for companionship, for membership in their clubs, etc. The result was as was to be expected. The Negro came last, with the American Indian being considered nearly three times more desirable, the figures being 2.05 for the Indian as against .97 or less than 1 per cent, for the Negro.

But the matter did not end there. Dr. Schlorff organized the students who voted against Negroes into special groups, and taught them something of the general history and background of the Negro, with the result that when he next questioned them more than twice as many considered the Negro desirable.

Now here is something that ought to make our Negro leaders, in particular, think and think deeply.

The so-called Negro is not only a minority in this country, but he is, on the whole, a poverty-stricken one. Three White men alone - Ford, Rockefeller and Mellon - are richer than 13,000,000 Aframericans combined. No matter how you look at it in the final analysis the Aframerican is dependent upon Whites for employment, on which, in turn, depends his social life and progress. Does it not seem, therefore, a matter of the most ordinary intelligence that the Negro should endeavor to acquaint the Whites with his good points and his history in particular?

The most vital fact to America as a nation is the winning of its independence. Now, if it were generally known that the first to lay down his life for this independence was a Negro, would not that alone make a great difference in the attitude of the Whites? Again, the fact that, according to no less an authority than Abraham Lincoln, it was the Negro who provided the balance of power that saved the Union in the Civil War! Or that, in the last war, the Negro was the group most to be trusted in this nation to the extent that he was set to safeguard the life of the Chief Executive and to watch over the munition plants? But how many White persons know this? And what is far worse, how many Negroes? But most have heard of the Emperor Jones.

Leaders Blamed for Conditions

And right here is where Negro leadership is to be blamed. Looking at it in its most charitable light at least 80 per cent of the present Negro leadership is futile. It leads the people nowhere, save to taking their money. Noise, noise, noise! Empty, outworn chatter that all save the lowest class of Whites outgrew forty years ago! Some of the followers, it is true, whoop and holler and feel joyful for the moment. But the effect is precisely that of water set to boil. When the fire is withdrawn and it has cooled off, it is always the same water. No progress has been made whatever.

Next to earning a living, the Negro's greatest care should be to learn the history of his racial group, and having learned it do all he can to impart it to the Whites, who, in turn, will have a higher opinion of him and be led to accord him the higher position that his more than 400 years of hard work in the upbuilding of this nation deserves.

Important to Learn Negro History

Nothing, nothing is more important than a knowledge of one's history. The history of any people is to them what memory is to the individual. The more advanced a people the greater attention they pay to their history, and the more they display it advantageously because they realize that it is like what dress and cosmetics are to a woman or a show window to a merchant.

But just because a knowledge of their history is vital and beneficial, it is difficult to get Negroes interested in it. Even in the so-called center of Negro culture, Harlem, I doubt strongly whether it would be possible to get as few as 100 persons to take a permanent interest in Negro history. About some obscure and irrelevant personage as David, Jehoshaphat, Jeremiah or King Solomon, most Negroes, however, know everything, but of Frederick Douglass, to whom they owe more than anyone else their American citizenship, they know little save the name, and many not even that. As long as most Negroes are more interested in jazz, in clowning on the pulpit and on the stage, dancing, card parties, social show-offs, hocus-pocus formula in lodges and other things of the moment than substantial knowledge, just so long they should cease blaming the Whites as the chief cause of their ills. More and more the Negro's economic and social salvation, which is the only salvation worth speaking of, is being dependent on himself. As to the leadership, people usually have the kind of leaders they deserve.

Yet, it seems to me that the merest common sense dictates that the example set by Dr. Schlorff should be followed by our Negro leaders. But that means, of course, that the majority of these leaders will have to learn something about the history of their group. So many mouth: "I love my race." Let them show that love by learning something about their race.

There are also those who believe that some coming revolution is going to bring the Negro into his own. We have had two revolutions already and both left the Negro almost where he was, because he was uneducated and unprepared; the third will find him the same. Were color prejudice to cease entirely in America tomorrow, the vast majority of Negroes would remain just where they are, not only because they are uneducated and unprepared, but because they are more interested in non-essentials than in those more solid and lasting things which cause the Whites to be on top.

The day seems far distant when scholars such as Arthur Schomburg, Carter G. Woodson, William Leo Hansberry, Willis N. Huggins and others, who have devoted a lifetime to digging out facts that give Negroes a better social and economic standing, will receive the acclaim that the mere charmers of words and phrases do now. Yet, stranger things have happened. In any case it is difficult to believe that the next generation of Negroes will be so uncritical, so gullible, so carried away by mere words and emptiness as is this one.

Rambling Ruminations

By J. A. ROGERS

A Colored Nation Gains Supremacy

Buried away in the financial section of the newspaper of October 4 is a news item which contains a lesson of the highest importance for those nations with a color-line.

This news is that Japan has at last wrested supremacy in the cotton exporting trade from England, although Britain had a start of nearly a century. For the first eight months of 1933 Japan exported 1,392,000,000 square yards of cotton cloth as against England's 1,386,000,000.

It was cotton more than any other commodity that gave world supremacy in commerce to Britain prior to the world war. So vital was cotton manufacture to England that although she was the foremost opponent of slavery she supported the South in the Civil War, lent millions to some of the seceding states, and built a warship for the South that played havoc with Northern shipping for a long time, and all of this because the South was supplying her with cotton.

And now this mighty nation has lost to little Japan, which less than thirty years ago was counted as one of the so-called inferior countries. Why has Japan won? This can be clearly traced.

One day in 1894 a tiny, dark-Colored man with a thin, sloping nose and thick lips, who would have passed unnoticed as a so-called Negro in any large Colored community in America, except that he was wearing a turban, was on a train in Natal,

South Africa, to which country he had just arrived. This man had a first-class ticket, but the conductor ordered him off to the Jim Crow compartment in the baggage car. When he refused the conductor stopped the train and shoved him out high on the mountains into the bitter cold night.

A few days later this Colored man, while walking innocently on a sidewalk in Pretoria, was pounced on by two burly policemen, who kicked and cuffed him severely, pitched him into the roadway, and warned him to walk there in the future as the sidewalk was reserved for Whites. The man that had been so brutally treated was Mohandas K. Gandhi.

England Feels Weight of Little Lawyer

Gandhi, who had been trained as a lawyer in England, had come to South Africa to plead a civil suit for one of his countrymen. This initiation into color prejudice stirred him as nothing else could have done, and he developed into a foe of England that was more effective than ten armies.

This shrewd little Black man decided to attack England in that part of her conscience where it would hurt most—namely, her pocketbook. India was England's greatest customer for cotton goods. Gandhi now urged his people to spin their own cloth. "Get out your spinning wheels as generations of your forefathers have done, " he said. And millions obeyed him.

Soon the result made itself felt in England. Great cotton mills in Lancashire, which had been running night and day for a century, closed by the hundreds, while the shipping and the railroads and other lines engaged in this trade suffered proportionately. Hundreds of thousands of workmen were thrown into the street; with their wives and children they found themselves without bread, and the government was forced to tax the population to give them a dole.

And as a result of that attack on Gandhi, the worst is yet to come, perhaps. England may lose India, which with its 350,000,000 population—three times greater than ours—is to the British Empire what the rest of the United States is to New York City. Great empires today are only huge cash registers. Lose India and Britain will be another Spain. And to this we'll say hurrah, for England is the bulwark of color prejudice—it is she who introduced it into the United States; it is she who is the only country in Europe, today, where one is likely to be refused service on account of color.

Thanks to Gandhi's preachings India is now one of the largest exporters of raw cotton. By making her own goods she has thus given the lead to Japan over England.

This interesting fact may be noted about Gandhi in South Africa, by the way: When he arrived there he did not consider himself a Colored man. In relating the incidents in his autobiography it will be noted that he has "coloured" in inverted commas. He was a high-caste Indian and no doubt thought himself superior to the Colored natives, although Negroid ancestry is evident among a large proportion of even the Brahmins. Millions of Negroids still exist in India, which might have been the home of the African Negro. But Gandhi, even with his turban, was but a Colored man to the arrogant Whites, with the result that they treated him just as any other Black native. Thus Destiny has her own way of bringing about her ends. Later, Gandhi seemed to have realized his kinship with the Natal Negroes, for when they revolted against the Whites in 1906 he served them most humanely as a stretcher bearer and medical attendant.

Race Prejudice Keeps All Down

England, it is evident, cannot win with the present treatment of her Colored subjects. And if she can't neither can America. It cannot be denied that the effort made in this country to keep down the Black man has been a factor of no small importance in causing its present economic plight. I have sat in the galleries of Congress and have seen for days at a time Southern congressmen sidetrack the pressing affairs of the nation to berate the Negro and block legislation simply because Negroes would be benefitted by it. And the same thing was going on in the Southern State Legislatures. In 1926, Virginia devoted three months to passing anti-Negro legislation with regard to so-called intermarriage; and an equally long period in 1928. Was there a bill introduced for the general welfare of the people, they viewed it through the spectacles of color, and if it contained any good for the Negro then it was bad for the nation.

Rambling Ruminations

By J. A. ROGERS

Says Abyssinian Are Not Anti-Negro

With regard to the discussion of why the Ras Desta Demtu did not call on the Aframerican brother while in the United States, it is my opinion that almost all of what I have seen so far of this discussion, including an article by Theophilus Lewis, has little or nothing to do with the real subject. Mr. Lewis' article, moreover, reads as if it were written by a professional Nordic, though it has, here and there, some excellent reasoning.

Some years ago, when an Ethiopian delegation headed by the Ras Naidu arrived in America, it fraternized too freely with Colored Americans, and this after the White ethnologists had gone to so much trouble to prove that the Abyssinian were White people. The result was that the Ras Naidu was snubbed by the White Americans and thereby failed in his mission. The Ras Desta Demtu, as I have good reason to believe, profited by that lesson. Not that I believe that he, personally, has any prejudice against Aframericans. On the contrary, like most Abyssinian, he might very much prefer a Black American to a White one, for the Abyssinian do not like White people. They have had to battle with them too long in order to preserve their independence. As Count Gleichen, one of the few White men who have written the truth on Ethiopia, has said: "With the exception of the King and a few enlightened dignitaries, it may be said that no Abyssinian wishes for progress or civilization in any way. He hates a White man and is anxious to keep all Europeans out of his country."

The Aframerican has no standing in his own country.

He is a doormat for every White foreigner. Almost wholly without influence of any sort, and having to depend largely upon the efforts of White people to get even common justice for himself, he is quite naturally not courted by foreign peoples of his own so-called race and color. Were Aframericans a powerful factor in their own land I wager that they would have heard from Ras Desta Demtu.

* * *

Aframericans Get First Chance

Moreover, some years ago the Abyssinian government tried hard to get trained Aframericans in its employ and failed. I understand that Dr. Workonah Martin made two voyages to America for this purpose in vain, and finally had to take Hindus instead. In consequence, I heard that Dr. Martin entertains a very poor idea of Aframericans, for which reason I hesitated to call on him when I was at Addis Ababa. In any case, the Abyssinian government gave the Aframericans the first choice, but they failed to respond. Another very important factor: The present Abyssinian government, like the present Egyptian one, if it is to remain in power, must play, or pretend to play, the White man's game, at least to a certain extent. The late Menelik was a real African at heart, and insisted on the dominance of African customs at his court. His grandson, the deposed Emperor, Lidj Yassu, and still the best beloved of the Abyssinian masses, set up the cry, "Africa for the Africans," and tried to unite all the tribes about him to drive the Whites out of East Africa, but he was downed and made a prisoner.

Abyssinia, because of its position with regard to the Suez Canal and India, and most of all because it owns Lake Tsana, is of the highest political importance. The White man's future, not only in Africa, but in Asia, depends a great deal on Abyssinia, hence the Whites are anxious to prove that its black-skinned inhabitants are their blood-brothers in order to isolate them. In short, the present regime in Abyssinia is given the choice of whether it is going to consider itself White or Black. If it chooses Black it is going to be considered a menace to White supremacy.

Though I am a so-called Negro, when I was in the Sudan I found very quickly that I had to choose whether I was going to be a Black man or a White man, and that latter choice was thrust upon me as the natives with whom I fraternized thought it best not to be seen in public with me. They feared for both me and themselves. I ate at the White hotels, from which these natives were barred. What is true of me would also have been true of Mr. Lewis. Yet my sympathy was all with the natives. The same is true of the newly arrived Whites, who must either knuckle in with the oppressors or get out of Africa. Of course, it is all very easy to sit at home and spin logic of what should be, but it is entirely different when one has to face hard, cold facts, not to mention the heavy artillery, aeroplanes, guns and bombs that the White man has trained on all of Africa, including Abyssinia. Had the Ras Desta Demtu fraternized with Negroes in America he would have been immediately suspected. The Aframerican who tries to get into certain parts of Africa, especially those owned by England, will readily understand this.

* * *

Says That Jews Are Hated Minority

It is impossible to treat this subject profoundly in a short article. Would, also, that space permitted my touching on some of many inaccuracies in Mr. Lewis' article, not to mention the others. For instance, Lewis speaks of the supposed Jewish ancestry of the Abyssinian ruling class, and asks: "Why should a foreign Jew pay any special attention to Negro communities unless he was looking for the easiest place to sell something." The only merit of this is that it sounds clever. The ruling Abyssinian tribes pride themselves on their Christianity, and would be offended if called Jews. The Jews, or Falashas, a Negroid tribe that once ruled the land, are a people apart and here, as elsewhere, there is no love lost between Christian and Jew.

Moreover, there is strong anthropological evidence that the Jews were originally a so-called Negro race. This reminds me that another writer declared that Ras Desta Demtu, while ignoring the Aframericans found time for company with the Jacobys. Mr. Jacoby was American Special Ambassador to Ethiopia for the coronation, and as such had met the Ras Demtu there. But the singular fact is this: certain Americans—and I overheard them myself at Addis-Ababa—objected to Mr. Jacoby, who, by the way, I found to be a most excellent gentleman, on the ground that he looked too much like a Colored man. He is Jewish, I believe. I heard one newspaper reporter ask why hadn't America chosen a real American to represent her.

* * *

Is Black White or White Black?

At first glance I myself thought Mr. Jacoby was Colored just as I did in the case of Theodore Roosevelt, Jr. Both may have had Negro ancestors generations ago. But the rich humor of the situation to me was that here were certain Americans calling the comparatively fair-skinned Mr. Jacoby "Colored" and the black-skinned woolly-haired Ethiopians as White.

Abyssinia, says Mr. Lewis, was the last country to hold on to legal slavery. The fact is that slavery, legal and illegal, exists over nearly all Africa today, not to mention Arabia and other parts of Asia. Only last year the Archbishop of Canterbury and other high personages called on the British government to end slavery in its African dominions as a tribute to Wilberforce, the centenary of whose death was observed this year. Yet Abyssinia and Liberia are picked out as horrible examples. This is simply because they are self-governed.

It is probably also true, as Lewis says, that it is only the armed might of Europe that keeps the Africans from one another's throat. But the Europeans have not only massacred the Africans by the tens of millions, like Leopold of Belgium, but they bring the Africans to fight in Europe, where more of them are killed by machine-guns in one hour than in their tribal battles in a year. White rule in Africa has been far more of a curse than a benefit for the natives. Were it not for their climate they would have been exterminated long ago, like the American Indian.

Africans Slandered by Missionaries

The African has been greatly slandered, especially by missionary societies while passing the plate. The people who could create such art as is to be seen in the Congo Museum at Brussels or the Trocadero in Paris surely cannot be such terrible savages as the Nordic thinking Negroes have been trained to think.

Of course, the African, as Mr. Lewis says, has no concept of racial unity. Neither, for that matter, has the European. But, as the latter quickly learns it when he goes to the Colored man's land, so White oppression is slowly but surely teaching the African that, as an oppressed Black man, he has something in common. More, I have met Colored peoples of all kinds—Hindus, Egyptians, Chinese, Japanese, Cubans, Moroccans, Somalis, Haitians, Arabians, and others—and I have yet to meet one that was not race-conscious where the imperialistic Whites were concerned. All have felt the might of their heel. Race is a capitalistic concept. It is a myth. There are in reality only two kinds of humanity: the exploiter and the exploited. But White oppression in Colored men's lands has made race a reality. This reality is not going to be simply conjured away when the Whites begin to find it working against them, and wish to get rid of it. This latter fact even the Communists are beginning to realize.

Within recent years I have noted an increasing number of Negroes who, in the desire to show how liberal and emancipated they are, feel that they must talk as if they were Nordics.

Rambling Ruminations

By J. A. ROGERS

Introduces Dunbar To the Sorbonne

PARIS—M. Louis T. Achille, instructor of French at Howard University, who is here on a leave of absence, recently presented to the graduate students in English at the Sorbonne a thesis on the 'Life and Poetical Works of Paul Laurence Dunbar," which was enthusiastically received. The professors of the University in particular, welcomed what is perhaps the first introduction of this great poet of Negro descent to the French public, and were warm in praise of it.

M. Achille, who is preparing the thesis for his doctor's degree, was asked to give wide circulation to his study of Dunbar and is now preparing it in French for the Revue Anglo-Americaine. M. Achille thought that Dunbar was far too little known in America, even among Aframericans.

The teacher was also one of the principal speakers at the annual meeting of the Association of Catholic University Laymen for Mission Work held at Rheims, France. At this gathering, which was attended by more than thirty races and nationalities, M. Achille read a report upon American color prejudice and segregation, which was widely discussed. All the speakers were in condemnation of the practice that denied human rights to the Aframericans, as well as to Negroes in certain parts of Africa.

One result of his address was the passing of a resolution for the purpose of intensifying plans to aid in the solution of the racial problem. Groups will be formed in all the countries to serve the Negroes, with no purpose of imposing Western civilization on them, the idea being rather to help them to develop along the lines of their own culture, but at the same time to strive for interracial understanding and brotherhood.

These European Catholics say that they expect to be either ignored or opposed by other Europeans of the old mentality in the colonies, but hope to win over the natives by kindly deeds. The association has received much encouragement from Pope Pius XI and the French clergy.

In honor of the new interracial friendships that had been formed, bottles of champagne were passed around, and Negro spirituals, African songs, and the folk-songs of the various nations represented were sung.

* * *

Ethiopian Envoy Travels Incognito

PARIS—The Ras Desta Damtou envoy and son-in-law of the Emperor Haile Selassie, is in this city strictly incognito, on a sight-seeing tour. In his flowing Ethiopian costume he has not been able to avoid the curious crowds and the photographers, however. One of his first acts on arriving here was to visit the Vaugirard Cemetery to place a wreath on the tomb of Paul Doumer, late president of France. When Ras Desta visited Paris in 1924 with Haile Selassie, Doumer had received him kindly and entertained him.

* * *

Prejudice Abroad

PARIS—Those Negroes who believe that the White race everywhere is afflicted with color prejudice are likely to find little consolation in the following incident which happened recently on the terrace of a Monteparnasse café. It is an international café, and one may find there Germans, Swedes, Norwegians, Poles, Egyptians, etc., and French, of course.

Among those seated there sipping their coffee or liqueurs was a very dark African with his companion, a White girl. As it happened one of the few vacant tables was beside this couple, and when an American and his feminine companion arrived the waiter escorted them thither.

At the sight of the Negro, the American not only refused to sit, but said angrily: "I'll be damned if I'll sit beside a black Nigger," while the woman said: "The idea of bringing us here. Let him find us another table."

The African, who understood English, at once exploded in excellent French, telling the American that he must remember that he was not in New York now, but in a civilized land. As soon as those at the adjoining table understood what it was all about they joined with the African in hooting the color-prejudiced American. One White woman shouted: "You can't come to Paris and lynch Negroes as you do at Scottsboro." Other tables took up the hooting and the whistling against the pair, and kept it up until the two disappeared in the crowd on the sidewalk.

This writer told of a similar incident that happened some three years ago when a White merchant from Oklahoma City with a Jewish name left his seat and came on the dance-floor to stop Benglia, the famous Senegalese dancer, dancing with a White Russian movie-star, in Benglia's own cabaret. On this occasion the Oklahoma City merchant was also razzed by the other dancers, nearly all of whom were White.

Rambling Ruminations

By J. A. ROGERS

Japan and Ethiopia Plan to Join Hands

Radio and press reports state that Prince Lij Araya, nephew of Emperor Haile Selassie of Ethiopia, may marry a Japanese noblewoman next May. The reports say that the union will be one step in an important political and economic mission.

The prince has selected two candidates from the photographs of ten young women of prominent and wealthy Japanese families. The choice will be made when he visits Japan shortly, according to a Japanese attorney who describes himself as the agent of the Abyssinian royal family.

The Ethiopian royalty traces its ancestry back some 5,000 years. When the Greeks, the first of the so-called White race, were emerging from barbarism, the Ethiopians and the Chinese had been civilized for more than 3,000 years.

Recent news dispatches also stated that Abyssinian land has been given to the Japanese for the growing of cotton, and that Japan now supplies Ethiopia with most of her cotton goods.

A growing bond of sympathy among the darker peoples of the world is inevitable under present conditions. Far-seeing students of the racial situation, as the late Sir Harry Johnson, have long been pointing this out. Each of these darker groups has some cause for complaint. I recall that on the ship on which I went to East Africa there were six of us of the darker race: an

Egyptian, an East Indian, an Abyssinian, a Chinese, a Japanese, and myself. All of us drifted to the same table, and the burden of our conversation was the injustice or the arrogance of the so-called White race towards our respective groups. The Chinese, who was a merchant, told for instance of the color line that the English, principally, had established in his country, after it had not known one in the 5,000 years of its previous history. As soon as these different oppressed groups undergo an interchange of thought and experience, the Whites living among them will have to change their tactics or they will get a dose of what the revolted slaves of Haiti under Biassou, Bouckman and Jean-Francois gave the Whites in 1791.

* * *

Color Bias in Black Africa

It is true that such White or near-White nations as France, Italy and Portugal have a minimum of color prejudice in their colonies. But under English and American pressure they are sometimes forced to it. For instance, Portuguese East Africa reeks with color discrimination through commercial compulsion from the adjoining British South Africa, while in Angola, or Portuguese West Africa a Black man receives the same treatment as in Portugal. France's treatment of the Black man in France has long offended the English and the Americans. Germany, most likely in the hope of winning English and American sympathy, is now launching a heavy attack on France because of her lack of color discrimination. Hitler is devoting much space in his official newspaper to this, and a recent issue carried copious photographs of Whites and Blacks of both sexes fraternizing or dancing together in Paris.

The mention of marriage between a Japanese and an Ethiopian will also cause a racial flutter among Americans, regardless of color, so rapped are they in the stupid and entirely false belief that race is a matter to be worried about. Next to birth and death, race-mixing is perhaps the most evident fact in human life. All peoples, no matter how pure they seem, are mixed. The darkest race was once very likely White, and the whitest race was once Black. Race-mixing and climate brought the change about. In any case it is surely easier to accept this theory than that a man came from an ape-like ancestor, as most of the leading scientists believe. When Europe was a tropical land the Negroes lived there. Indeed, all other varieties of mankind, as the Chinese and Japanese, seem to have originated from a union of the Black and the White varieties of the human race.

There is a moral in all of this for the Aframerican. Let him toss out of his brain all the Hebrew mythology and all Nordic doctrine of supposed inferiority that now fills it. In its place let him absorb modern thought so that when the time comes he may be able to demand a place in the sun, instead of being shifted off, willy-nilly, to the labor of battalions as in the last war.

Rambling Ruminations

By J. A. ROGERS

Kelly Miller's Back to Farm Plan

Prof. Kelly Miller of Howard University is requesting the national government to send the Negroes in large cities "back" to the farms, suggesting that the money spent in relief would be much better used thus. The New York Herald Tribune, editorially, heartily agrees with Professor Miller.

At this time a policy of sending the unemployed back to the soil—not only the Negroes but the Whites as well—appears to be fundamentally sound. But circumstances do alter cases.

Let us look at the proposition, pro and con. First, there can be little doubt that Western civilization is on the decline. It is built upon commerce and in this the Western nations are losing out to the Eastern ones. Only this week appeared a significant news item that "Japan's increase of commerce in half a year of 56.3 per cent lead the world." On the other hand, the United States showed a decline of 19.9 per cent; Germany 40.4; Czecho-Slovakia 28.8; France 10.9 and Great Britain, 6.3. In short, while Japan's foreign trade increased, that of the great manufacturing nations of a decade ago declined. The trade of the Indian Ocean once in the hands of these European nations is now controlled by Asiatics. In Abyssinia, for instance, America once led in cotton cloth to the extent that this cloth was known as "Americani." Now the cotton cloth sold there is made by Asia.

The Western nations with their higher cost of production cannot hope to compete with the Eastern ones, and as time goes on the former are sure to lose still more of their trade, thus becoming weaker and weaker. And if the West ever goes to war with the East over trade it will be too bad for the West.

Urban populations depend upon trade. During the war and soon after the urban population of this nation increased until it exceeded the rural. Industry called millions away from the farm, and now that there is no work for them—and even at the risk of being called a pessimist I will say that there is never going to be any, for America is now paralleling the case of England—it seems that the logical thing for them is to go back to the soil.

But logic is one thing and reality is quite another. The farmers in one-half the states of the Union are on strike because they are suffering terribly. They work hard and get almost nothing. Those city folks who are getting relief are much better off than the average farmer. How, then, is the sending of people back to the soil going to help the situation?

* * *

Machine Age Changes Things

Of course, this doctrine was good in the days of Jean Jacques Rousseau, and perhaps even in the days when professor Miller was on the farm. But in this day of machinery the small farmer meets the same competition as the small businessman. In other words, he has no chance against big business. Besides, is it not this same machinery that drove the people from the farms in the first place?

Again, the larger the city population is it not the better chance the farmers have to sell their produce? Take back to the soil any large proportion of the urban population and you at once reduce the farmer's market, thereby increasing his difficulties. Ah, no, this is a problem that cannot be solved by such a simple formula as that offered by Professor Miller.

Professor Miller might reply that he was speaking only of the Negroes, but surely he knows that the national government would know better than to select only Negroes. And as I said, it is clear that the "return" of even a half of the unemployed to the farms would increase competition enormously for the farmers.

The problem of the unemployed will, I believe, settle itself, but not in our generation, provided that there is some sort of birth control. But even this won't solve it, for naturally there will be less mouths to consume the farmer's products.

It seems to me that the only way out is for the government to assume control of all employment, that is, let the government be responsible that each man on the farm or in the city, gets work, and if not, then he must be fed. The haves must be taxed in order that the have-nots may eat.

* * *

Lynching and Labor

Professor Miller also suggests that his proposed Negro migrants to the farm should be sent to the South. This, in my opinion, would be woeful shortsightedness. One of the greatest evils in this nation is the color problem. It originates in the South. The virus of color prejudice in the South poisons the rest of the nation. Now, everyone knows that the migration of the Negro from the South during the war lessened the evil there. This migration was directly responsible for reducing lynching

80 per cent. Would Professor Miller send these Negroes again to the South to have an increase in lynching? The lynching problem in the South is directly connected with that of labor. The fewer the Negroes the greater the demand for their labor, and the more the employers are inclined to protect them from the mob. Increase the percentage of Negroes and you have the opposite situation, in proportion to the increase. No, instead of sending Negroes South, one should be finding ways of getting them out. Nothing so softens and humanizes the average Southerner to power as when his Negro worker and his Negro concubine are lacking. Are our memories so short that we cannot recall what took place in 1917-18 when the Negroes left in large numbers? If there must be a migration why not to states like Idaho, Washington and Oregon?

I disagree with most of what Professor Miller has said and consequently also the Herald Tribune's deductions. The chief merit of both is that the argument is plausible. Professor Miller also thinks that the rural Negro is healthier than the urban one. I am not so sure of this; moreover, the city Negro has much better opportunities to maintain a healthy body, thanks to greater medical facilities. And in the matter of education and general enlightenment there can be no comparison whatever. Professor Miller's view of the status of the city Negro is also far too narrow.

Nevertheless, as I said, it does seem to me that the settling on farms of the unemployed who wish to get back to nature is an excellent thing. But in the name of humanity do not send those Negroes who had the initiative and enterprise to get out of the South back there again. That, rather, is the place for the White unemployed. Boley is successful, it is true, but does that mean, Professor Miller, that a hundred Boleys certainly would be also?

For one thing, would the Southern Whites permit them? To believe they would is to ignore completely the economic determinant of color prejudice and lynching.

Rambling Ruminations

By J. A. ROGERS

The Glamour Of the Lowly

Recently, by way of boosting winter tours to the West Indies, a New York daily carried a picture of a number of Black boys of Kingston, Jamaica, grinning in a row and an old Black peasant woman smoking a long pipe, with the title: "Where Laziness Reigns." Some friends of mine from that island became highly indignant at it and were for writing to the editor, protesting that the types shown were not characteristic of the country, and inquiring why something of the better side of Jamaican life was not shown.

It was not shown for the simple reason that tourists wish to see something different when they travel, and the more difficult it is, the better. Moreover, the islanders are Colored and to have shown some of the highly-cultured, light-Colored folks there instead of the "pure" Negro type peasantry would have been an advertisement with a reverse pull.

The same is essentially true of the United States. The peasant Negro is vastly more interesting to the Whites than a Negro graduate from Yale or Harvard. Most of the books or reference to Negroes in books and magazines are about this kind of Negro. Indeed, the literary output on the peasant Negro has been enormous, and the public seems never to have enough of it.

It is inevitable that the Negro be written about. American life is extraordinarily flat and monotonous—a vast white desert, judging from the literary and the dramatic output on it.

The Negro adds color, physically and spiritually, to this life. He laughs, sings, jigs, makes music, and is content with the promise of eating pie in the sky by and by. Besides he is ostracized and booted, the knowledge of which helps immensely to make the White brother contented with his own lot. Nothing helps to give some folks a sense of well-being as learning that others are in trouble. As Mr. Dooley used to say so neatly, the height of comfort to him was to sit in the shade sipping iced lemonade and watch Italian laborers breaking rocks in the scorching sun. In short, the Negro exercises a great fascination on the White man. When one touches on the matter of sex this fascination is multiplied. In the good old days the Southern aristocrats used to meet the slave ships eagerly at the pier to see what new in the line of Black Venuses had arrived. Poems were written about them and I have an old picture showing a Black Venus being escorted from West Africa by a White Neptune and White Cupids.

Hence, a film as "The Emperor Jones" or one of the many darkies clowning in a picture helps to relieve the boredom of the White brother, fed up with himself and his civilization. I recall once hearing a famous White writer remark to a friend: "I'm fed up with this Anglo-Saxon whiteness." And there are many others like him.

* * *

Traditional Negro Will Live Long

As long as this monotony exists in White civilization the Negro is going to be featured on that side of his life of which he is least proud. And if every Negro were to become a paragon tomorrow it wouldn't make any difference. The traditional Negro would live on, for tradition is stronger than reality. Above all, the traditional Negro has a market value in the great field of amusement, while the Negro, as he actually is, is not worth a picayune to White promoters. And most likely to Negro audiences, too.

Since the Whites, as I said, are interested most in the humbler and the seamier side of Negro life, I forecast that we are going to have more of that and in progressively stronger doses. There is, for instance, the latest book on the Negro, "Kingdom Come," by Roark Bradford. I have not read this book, and do not need to, as I know Bradford's writings well. I have merely seen the review of it, and it sounds so much like Bradford's sensationalism that I quote a part of it, feeling sure that I am not doing him an injustice.

Speaking of the period just before the emancipation:

"Tragedies were inevitable and an officer announced that only women without babies could go. Some days later a huge mound of cotton, which had lain long near this landing awaiting shipment, was moved and the little black corpses of pickaninnies, pushed between bales by their mothers and left to die, fell out like rain."

* * *

Mr. Roark Bradford's Wonderful Babies

Far be it from me to call Mr. Bradford a liar with a short and ugly word added. Rather we are indebted to him for the discovery of two brand-new Negro characteristics: First, that Negro babies do not cry; and second, that they do not smell after they have lain dead for days in a hot climate. There were enough babies thrust behind those, we suppose, tightly-packed bales of cotton to have made a squalling that reached to New Orleans, and yet these well-behaved lambs just lay there for days and died without uttering a bleat. Well, if you cannot swallow that, just imagine that all the people about the landing, both immediately before and after the sailing of the boat, were all deaf.

* * *

German Nazis and Superiority Complex

Psychologists have coined the term "inferiority complex" to describe the minds of those who believe themselves inferior; and "superior complex" for those who look down on others. But like all definitions of this sort, they are true only within a certain narrow range. Negroes, for instance, are supposed to possess the former, and the Germans the latter. The Germans do not only believe themselves superior to all the dark-skinned varieties of mankind, but to all other Whites as well. And the Germans are, to a certain degree, superior. Illiteracy is almost nil among them; they are thorough in everything, and their country is perhaps the best kept one in Europe. All Germany, that is, the streets, etc. looks like a well-kept home. The Germans' excellence in medicine, science, philosophy, and music is well known. In general culture they are perhaps at the top.

But here's the contradiction. One of the marks of an inferiority complex, we are told, is an exaggerated notion of one's ancestral past. There's a saying: He who boasts of his ancestry is like a potato, for the best part of him is underground. When one manufactures a past, the inferiority complex becomes even more evident. And this is just what the Germans are doing. It is being taught now in Germany that the Germans are the originators of all learning and culture, and that the ancient Egyptians, for instance, were of Teutonic stock.

Now while the early history of the darker peoples is lost in the mist of antiquity, we know as surely as we can know anything just who and what the early Northern Europeans, and the Germans, in particular, were. Caesar, Tacitus, Velleius, Paterculus, Strabo and St. Jerome have left us an accurate description of them. We know that the Germans were the Congo savages of Caesar's day; that they were cannibals, great gluttons, that they drank the blood of their enemies, and that incest was common, at least among the Britons. In short, we writers of a darker color have the goods on the superior Nordic. Hence, Hitler, as an historian, still remains a good house painter.

Take the swastika, his emblem. It is more than 5,000 years old and originated so far as we know among the Negroid peoples of Oceania. It later found its way among the Red Indians. The Basques, who are the oldest race in Europe, and very probably descendants of the Negro aborigines of Europe, have been using the swastika as their national symbol for more than 2,000 years. This summer, in their shop windows, I saw signs stating this fact, and disclaiming any sympathy with the Nazis. Yet the impression in Germany is that Hitler, himself, designed the swastika, and so it might go down in German history.

* * *

Black Madonna and Christ in Bavaria

The so-called Negro also played an important part in civilizing primitive Germany. The first missionaries to that barbarian land, even before Caesar, were the Egyptians who carried the worship of Isis and Horus there. Today an important relic of this civilizing influence is to be seen at Alt-Otting in Bavaria, where the Black Isis and Horus are still worshipped under the guise of the Black Madonna and the Black Christ. This Negroid statue is the most popular Christian shrine in all Germany. In other parts of Southern Germany are to be found these Black Madonnas and Black Christs, all relics of Negro culture as busts of White Christ in Africa are signs of the White man's presence there. Truly Hitler's history is on a par with his Charlie Chaplin mustache.

Further, Germany's greatest celestial saint is pictured all over the land as a coal-black Negro with wooly hair, namely St. Maurice, or Mauritius. Maurice comes from Moor (Mohr, which is German for Negro). As I write I have before me a picture of this pure-type Negro from one of the German cathedrals and he is wearing the German eagle on his head, if you please. [***Editor's Note***: the statue is located in the Magdeburg Cathedral in Germany] Today, nine centuries later, Hitler is being shown in Germany also with this eagle on his head…

Rambling Ruminations

By J. A. ROGERS

Harlem Pickets Lack Glamour

In spite of the pickets pacing before certain stores on Harlem's 125th Street, because these places draw the color line in the matter of employment, Negroes in considerable numbers continue to patronize them.

At first thought this seems due to a total lack of racial self-respect on the part of the customers. On second thought, however, I have set it down rather as a failure on the part of the boycotters to employ the right tactics to draw attention to themselves.

First, the signs carried before the stores by the pickets lack pep. They are unattractive and say practically nothing. In a crowd few people notice them, and it is safe to say that only a small percentage of the people in Harlem have heard of this boycott.

* * *

Need for Ballyhoo

The signs should strike the on-comer at a glance. Since, as the Chinese say, one picture is worth ten thousand words, they should bear a cartoon with snappy words. If necessary the pickets should wear garb that would strike the eye even in a crowd.

No program, religious, political, social, literary, or what you will, was put over without ballyhoo. And the further down the people are in the social scale, the more this ballyhoo is necessary. No matter how worthy your program, to get people interested in it, you need plenty of noise. And this goes also for 99 per cent of the most supercilious intellectuals and radicals. Human nature is just built that way. For every one who will stop to listen to a violin played by the best master, ten thousand will run off to hear a drum just because it's more noisy.

* * *

Used for Oppression

I for one believe that all Negroes have some degree of racial self-respect, and that at bottom they're no different from Jews, Italians, Germans and others who certainly would never help to support anything that discriminated against them. But the Negro has been born in an atmosphere of oppression and has grown used to it as the offspring of a wild animal born in a cage is accustomed to confinement. Therefore he needs a lot of ballyhooing to get it out of him, something as was in the Garvey movement.

Every movement that ever rose to be anything was born in ballyhoo. Read the lives of the saints, for instance. They are probably the biggest collection of miracles, fairytales and downright deception ever told. Yet they drew simple-minded people into the Christian religion and helped to make it the power it is today. Someone has said: It is impossible to overestimate the stupidity of mankind. Common sense, refinement or impartial truth has never won any cause yet and probably never will as long as mankind remains what it is.

* * *

A Vital Step

What the boycotters are attempting is vital and can be made to attain a national significance that will probably go further than anything else to bring about a solution of the race problem. What we need in America is an erasing of the color line and the bringing about of a common citizenship such as exists in any other country. Blacks and Whites are here to stay as long as this remains America. And nothing can ever be gained by their pulling apart.

What the boycotters are doing has been due for a long time. It was inevitable. The Negro is bound to grow more self-respecting. Already one store—Koch's—has some sixty Negro clerks. If support is shifted to this store, provided one also feels he is getting his money's worth, the Jim Crow stores are bound to change sooner or later.

And in the meantime the boycotters need more pep in their tactics. With noisy advertisement you can sell anything to the American people, and that goes for the so-called Negro, too.

Rambling Ruminations

By J. A. ROGERS

Travel as an Education

It will be my pleasure to conduct a tour of the Mediterranean countries and Russia this summer.

Eleven countries, twenty cities and their environment will be visited. The party will sail on the Roma of the Italian Line on June 30, stopping at the delightful tropical island of Madeira, noted for its wine, and also at Gibraltar. This world-famed fortress, by the way, was named after a Negro slave, who rose to be conqueror of Spain. Both shores of the Mediterranean teem with the history of the so-called Negro, who at times dominated its azure waters with mighty Navies. A visit to Gibraltar alone is worth the trip to Europe.

* * *

To Visit Tomb of Christ

Malaga, Spain; Monte Carlo, famed in the world of chance; Monaco, a bare rock converted into an artificial paradise; Nice and other playgrounds of the cream of the world's wealth; Genoa, birthplace of Columbus, and Naples will be visited also. Naples is full of extraordinary interest with the historic volcano, Vesuvius, the excavated cities of Pompeii and Herculaneum, the Cathedral, and Blue Grotto of the island of Capri.

The itinerary includes also a stop at Taormina, Sicily and

a visit to its classic Greek and Roman ruins. At Beirut in Syria the mountains of Lebanon from which came the cedar for the building of Solomon's Temple; the mighty ruins of Baalbeck and other famed places will be seen. Three full days will be spent in Palestine seeing the noted places of Bible history—Jerusalem, the tomb of Christ, the River Jordan, etc. This part of the tour will be by auto car, which affords a close-up of the place and the people. For the sociologically-minded the people will be found even more interesting than the places.

* * *

Land of Soviets

Other stops in the Levant made by the Roma, will be Port Said, Egypt, at the head of the Suez Canal, and the Island of Rhodes, famed for its Colossus. En route to Russia, Constantinople will be toured. Three weeks will be spent in Russia where every opportunity will be afforded by the authorities to view at first hand what the Soviets are doing in their efforts to bring about a juster form of human society. Old Russia as well as new Russia will be seen together with the souvenirs of Pushkin, Negro poet, whose writings played the same part in liberating the White Russian slaves as those of Harriett Beecher Stowe the Black American ones.

* * *

Not a Philanthropist

From Russia the party will go by boat to London. While there arrangements will be made for those who wish to visit Paris. The cost of the tour which lasts sixty-seven days is $540. This includes everything save passport, visas, tips on the boats, and laundry. With no desire to pose as a philanthropist I may add that my services as conductor are free. And in order that all may be conducted in a business-like way the financial arrangements are placed in the hands of the well-known tourist agents. Paul Tausig & Sons, 29 West Forty-sixth Street, New York City. The Russian part of the tour is under the Open Road and the Intourist, the official government travel bureau. For many years I have been asked why I did not conduct a tour. This is the answer.

Recreation will be combined with education. Personally, I know of no more stimulating form of pleasure than travel. From a tour of this sort one will return with enough thrilling experiences to last a lifetime. Incidentally, next to the winning of a sweepstakes ticket, perhaps nothing so increases one's prestige among one's friends as a trip abroad. Better than all, however, is the larger and newer outlook it gives one on life. Return is on the Majestic arriving in New York, September 4.

Index

A

B

C

D

G

H

L

M

N

O

P

Q

R

T

U

V

W

Y

Also From Mind On The Matter Publishing

Dumbin' Down: Reflections on the Mis-Education of the Negro
by Jeff Menzise, Ph.D.
ISBN# 978-0-9856657

"Current and future generations of scholars will benefit from this work"
Safisha Nzingha Hill, Ph.D.

"His profound body of scholarship reflects the spirit, integrity & intellectual DNA of Dr. Carter G. Woodson's ageless thesis."
Alfred "Coach" Powell

"No social activist, educator or parent who is serious about the well-being of Black children should miss this read."
Carol Brunson Day, Ph.D.

www.ingramcontent.com/pod-product-compliance
Lightning Source LLC
Chambersburg PA
CBHW060607310726
48982CB00008B/1264/J

* 9 7 8 0 9 8 5 6 6 5 7 1 5 *